AN INTEGRATED
APPROACH TO SIGHTSINGING

RHYTHM
AND
PITCH

JOHN R. STEVENSON

MARJORIE S. PORTERFIELD

RHYTHM AND PITCH

AN INTEGRATED APPROACH TO SIGHTSINGING

John R. Stevenson
Marjorie S. Porterfield

Ithaca College

PRENTICE-HALL, INC.   *Englewood Cliffs, New Jersey 07632*

Library of Congress Cataloging-in-Publication Data

STEVENSON, JOHN R., (date)
  Rhythm and pitch.

  1. Sight-singing. 2. Rhythm. 3. Musical intervals
and scales. I. Porterfield, Marjorie S., (date).
II. Title.
MT870.S827 1986   784.9'4   85-3551
ISBN 0-13-780743-0

Editorial/production supervision and
  interior design: Lisa A. Domínguez
Cover design: Debra Watson
Manufacturing buyer: Ray Keating

Printed in the United States of America

10 9 8 7 6 5 4 3 2 1

0-13-780743-0   01

Prentice-Hall International (UK) Limited, *London*
Prentice-Hall of Australia Pty. Limited, *Sydney*
Prentice-Hall Canada Inc., *Toronto*
Prentice-Hall Hispanoamericana, S. A., *Mexico*
Prentice-Hall of India Private Limited, *New Delhi*
Prentice-Hall of Japan, Inc., *Tokyo*
Prentice-Hall of Southeast Asia Pte. Ltd., *Singapore*
Editora Prentice-Hall do Brasil, Ltda., *Rio de Janeiro*
Whitehall Books Limited, *Wellington, New Zealand*

CONTENTS

Rhythm and Pitch: An Integrated Approach to Sightsinging represents an attempt by the authors to formulate a music reading text that incorporates a gradual increase in difficulty in both pitch and rhythm study. Too often, difficult rhythmic elements are incorporated much too early in the study of music reading. In this text, the material is carefully coordinated to emphasize the building of basic skills in the areas of both pitch and rhythm before moving on to the next level of difficulty.

Each unit in this text contains:

1. an explanation of the rhythmic elements which will be found in the unit.
2. an explanation of the melodic elements which will be found in the unit.
3. various pitch exercises to strengthen skills in those elements.
4. various rhythm exercises with suggestions for practice and performance.
5. melodies for sightsinging that incorporate melodic and/or rhythmic elements both from the current unit and preceding units.

Many units contain two-part rhythmic and melodic examples.

RHYTHM: *The Beat (First Division and First Multiple)*
PITCH: *Major and Minor Seconds; The Major Scale*
CLEFS: *Treble and Bass*

RHYTHM: *The Beat (First Division and First Multiple)*

The *beat* or *pulse* is a musical phenomenon inherent in Western music. It is recognized instinctively as a series of continuous oscillations which recur at predetermined time intervals.

The tempo (or speed) of the beat is usually determined by listening to the culmination of several musical elements, i.e. harmonic rhythm, melodic contour, and, in some cases, articulation.

In this unit the student should listen to various music examples in simple meter, identifying the tempo of the beat and clapping that beat at tempo primo, then twice as fast or twice as slow. It would also be beneficial to tap tempo primo with one hand and with the other hand tap either twice as fast or twice as slow. Exercises can be devised whereby, upon a given verbal command (such as "change"), the student can switch between hands, switch from twice as fast to twice as slow, or return to tempo primo.

In rhythm notation the note value that is chosen to match the impulse of the beat is considered to be the *beat-note value.* Beat-note values in this unit are quarter notes, eighth notes, or half notes.

Multiple (twice as slow)	𝅗𝅥	𝅘𝅥	𝅝
Beat-note value (tempo primo)	𝅘𝅥 𝅘𝅥	𝅘𝅥𝅮 𝅘𝅥𝅮	𝅗𝅥 𝅗𝅥
Division (twice as fast)	𝅘𝅥𝅮𝅘𝅥𝅮 𝅘𝅥𝅮𝅘𝅥𝅮	𝅘𝅥𝅯𝅘𝅥𝅯 𝅘𝅥𝅯𝅘𝅥𝅯	𝅘𝅥 𝅘𝅥 𝅘𝅥 𝅘𝅥

PITCH: *Major and Minor Seconds; The Major Scale*

An *interval* is the distance between two tones. Intervals have two properties: size and quality. The *size* of an interval is determined by the number of different pitch names the interval encompasses and is expressed as an arabic numeral. For example, from C to D would be a *second*, encompassing the two different pitches C→D, C to E would be a third [C→D→E→], C to A a sixth [C→D→E→F→G→A], and so on. The following example illustrates the different sizes of intervals within an octave.

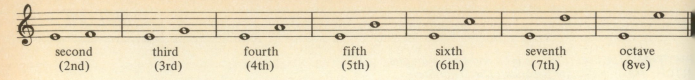

second | third | fourth | fifth | sixth | seventh | octave
(2nd) | (3rd) | (4th) | (5th) | (6th) | (7th) | (8ve)

Intervals of the same size (for example, sixths) may have different *qualities* depending on the number of half steps in the various intervals. The different qualities are: major (M), minor (m), perfect (P), diminished (O), and augmented (+). Intervals that are seconds, thirds, sixths, or sevenths may be major or minor. Intervals that are unisons (having the same note name and pitch), fourths, fifths, or octaves may be perfect. Any interval may be augmented or diminished.

The following chart shows the relationship of the various qualities of intervals to each other.

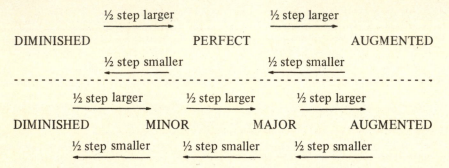

Unit 1 presents material on the interval of the *second*. The smallest musical interval is the minor second (m2), or *half step*. If one visualizes a keyboard, a half step is the distance between one key and the next closest black or white key. On the illustration below, the arrows [◄——►] show all possible half steps on the given keyboard.

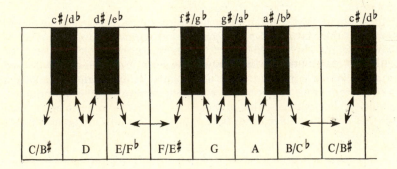

The next larger interval in size, the major second (M2), or *whole step,* can be thought of as consisting of two half steps. The next illustration shows major seconds on the same keyboard.

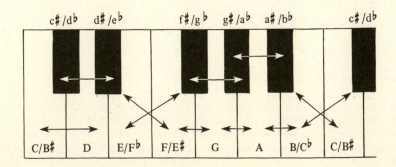

The *major scale* is a series of eight consecutive pitches. These eight pitches will always consist of the same sequence of major and minor seconds, resulting in the characteristic sound of the major scale. There are half steps between the third and fourth scale degrees and the seventh and eighth scale degrees and whole steps between the others. The following example illustrates two different major scales.

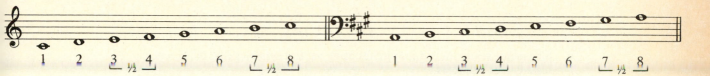

Units 1 through 5 contain melodic material that is limited to the use of the major *mode*. That is, the melodies use notes contained in the major scale. The keynote (or first note) of any major scale will be referred to as *tonic*. This note will be the focus of any piece of tonal music. Tonic of any melody can be determined by many factors:

1. It is often the first or last note.
2. It is often the highest or lowest note.
3. It is often the longest or most frequent note.
4. The notes of the *tonic triad* (1 3 5 of the scale) are used often in the melody.

Although some of the pitch exercises involve drill with intervals out of a tonal context, the pitch patterns and melodies will all be in a major tonality.

Before beginning the pitch exercises, practice singing and identifying major and minor seconds. To gain proficiency in singing minor seconds, sing a pitch and then sing the closest note above or below that pitch. To practice major seconds, sing the first two notes of a major scale, ascending (1-2) or descending (2-1).

PITCH EXERCISES:
Major and Minor Seconds

1. At the piano, play each note *where written,* match the pitch in your own vocal range and sing: a) a minor second above each note, b) a minor second below each note, c) a major second above each note, and d) a major second below each note.

2. Play and match each pitch as above and sing the designated interval above or below the given note. Use a neutral syllable (da, ba, la, etc.) and/or pitch names.

3. Play the given pitch. Then sing the given progression of intervals in the directions indicated. You should end up on the given last pitch.

given pitch: C ↑M2 ↓m2 ↑M2 ↑m2 ↑M2   last pitch: F♯
given pitch: F ↓m2 ↓m2 ↓M2 ↑m2 ↑M2   last pitch: E
given pitch: C ↑M2 ↑M2 ↑m2 ↓M2 ↓m2   last pitch: D
given pitch: G ↓m2 ↓M2 ↓M2 ↑m2 ↑M2   last pitch: F
given pitch: E ↑m2 ↓M2 ↓m2 ↓M2 ↑m2   last pitch: D♭

4. Sing major scales on various pitches using neutral syllables (da, ba, la, etc.) and scale degree numbers.
5. Establish the given key by singing the tonic triad on the numbers 1 3 5 3 1. Then sing the given pattern on scale degree numbers.

D major: 1 2 3 4 5 6 5 4 5 4 3 2 1 7 1
E♭ major: 3 4 5 4 3 2 1 2 1 2 3 4 5 6 5
F major: 5 4 3 2 3 4 5 4 3 2 1 7 1 2 1
G major: 3 2 1 7 1 2 3 4 5 6 5 4 3 2 1
A♭ major: 1 7 1 7 6 5 6 7 1 2 3 4 3 2 3

PITCH PATTERNS

Play the tonic pitch and establish tonic by singing scale degree numbers 1 3 5 3 1. Then sing the given patterns on neutral syllables (la, ba, da, etc.), scale degree numbers, pitch names, or solfeggio syllables.

RHYTHM READING

On each exercise perform the tasks in the order given while clapping the assigned beat-note value. Use a variety of tempi and dynamics.

1. Articulate the rhythm on neutral syllables (da, ba, la, etc.).
2. Improvise a major melody using a variety of intervals and end on tonic. Use a variety of tonalities.
3. Improvise a major melody using only major and minor seconds and end on tonic. Use a variety of tonalities.

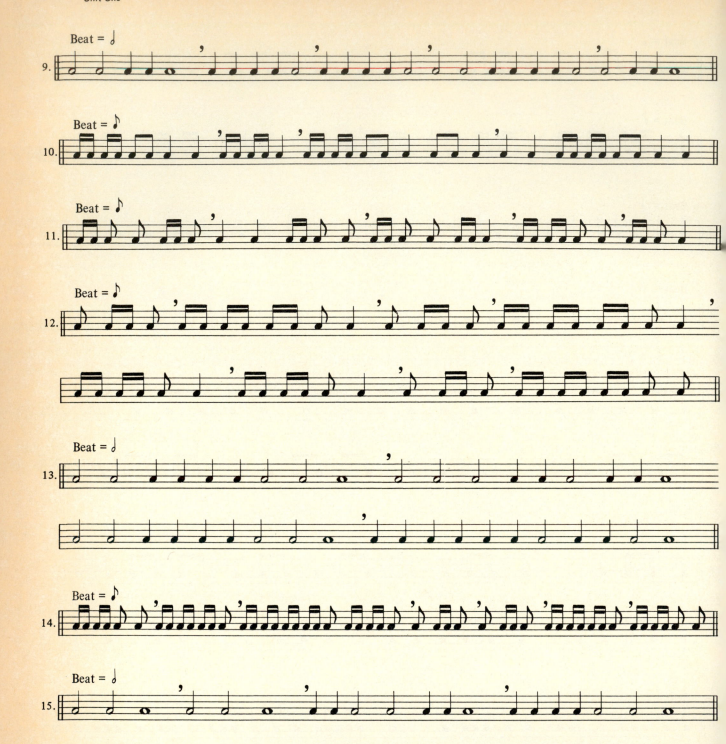

CLEF READING

On each exercise perform the tasks in the order given while clapping the assigned beat-note value. Use a metronome, beginning at a slow tempo and increasing the rate of speed daily. Invent your own articulation for exercises that are unedited.

1. Speak the rhythm on syllables that will produce the desired articulation.
2. Speak (not sing) the letter name of each note out loud in the designated clefs in proper rhythm while observing the correct articulation.

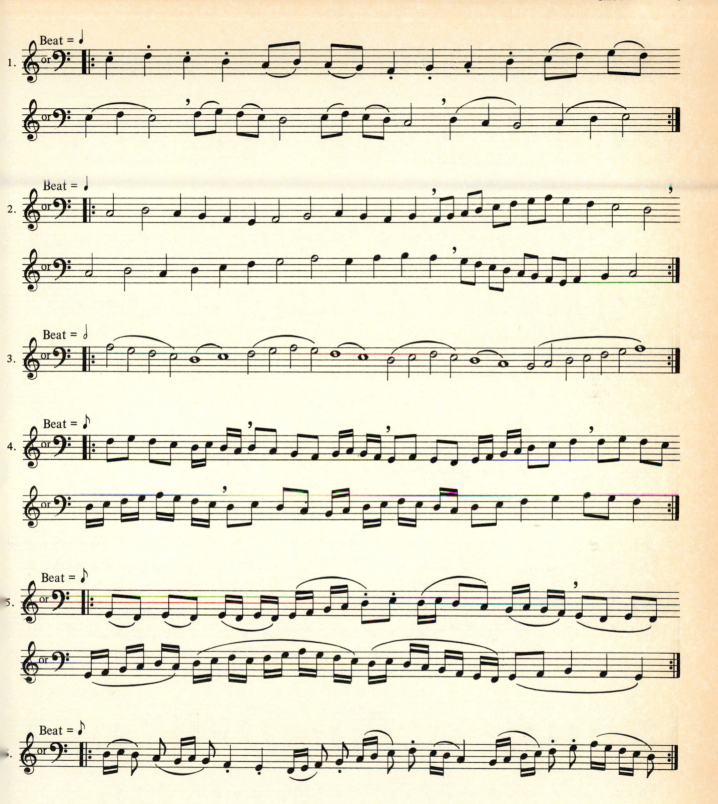

MELODIES

Establish the tonic and the beat. While clapping the beat, sing the melodies on neutral syllables (da, ba, la, etc.), then with scale degree numbers, solfeggio syllables, and finally with pitch names.

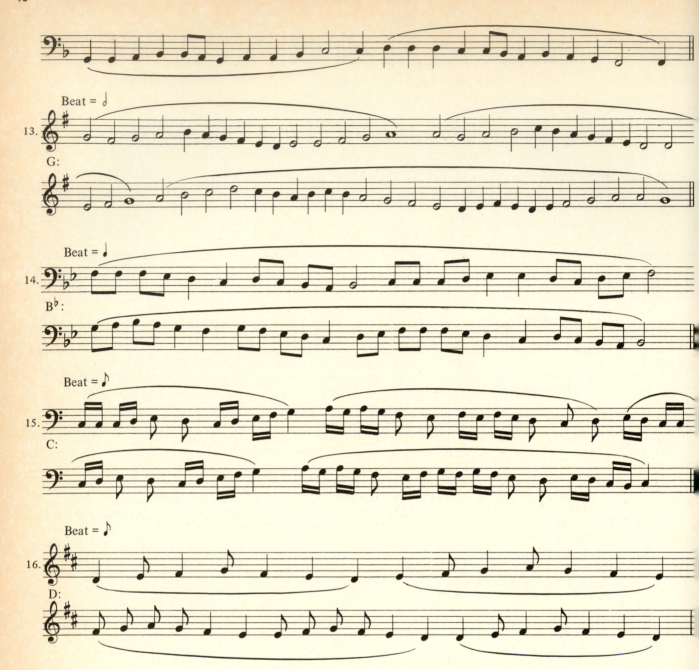

RHYTHM: *Simple Meter (Duple, Triple, and Quadruple)*
PITCH: *Major and Minor Thirds; Triads*
CLEFS: *Treble and Bass*

RHYTHM: *Simple Meter (Duple, Triple, and Quadruple)*

METER

Meter is the result of the structuring of beats into a recurring series of stresses. Each series is known as a measure. Each stress in the measure is of a different character. The first stress type in any given series is called the *crusis*. The *crusic stress* is the most dominant in the measure and is perceived instinctively. The last stress type in any measure is called the *anacrusis*. The *anacrusic stress* evokes the sensation of preparation. This stress is easily identified on paper, for it is always followed by a vertical bar known as a *bar line*. Any additional beats within a measure exist between the crusis and the anacrusis. These middle beats are known as *metacrusic stresses*. The metacruses act as bridges from the crusis to the anacrusis. In any given measure, therefore, there is one crusis, one anacrusis, and any number of metacruses. Once the number of stresses in each measure has been established, then the meter signature can be notated.

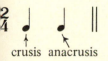
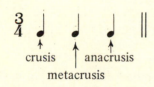
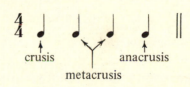

SIMPLE BINARY METERS

The first two meters covered in this unit contain an even number of beats and therefore the measure can be divided naturally into two equal portions or sides. Because of this characteristic, these meters are referred to as *binary meters*.

The binary meter that contains two beats uses the arabic numeral 2 as the top figure in its meter signature. In a 2 meter, one side of the measure contains the crusic beat and the other side contains the anacrusic beat. The binary meter that contains four beats uses the arabic numeral 4 as the top figure in its meter signature. In a 4 meter, one side of the measure contains a crusic and a postcrusic metacrusic beat while the other side contains a preanacrusic metacrusic beat and an anacrusic beat (in that order).

The beat in these meters is assigned a given note value, which is employed to represent its duration. In this unit the note values used are those that can be naturally divided by two. They are [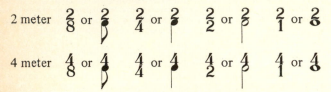]. The act of dividing a note value by two is known as *simple division*. If a given meter employs simple division, it is a *simple meter*. Traditionally, the simple beat-note values are represented in the meter signature by arabic numerals. For example: the eighth note [♪] is represented by the numeral 8; the quarter note[♩] is represented by the numeral 4; the half note [𝅗𝅥] is represented by the numeral 2. These numerals are the bottom figures in the signature. Therefore, the terms binary and simple are used to describe meter in two ways. The term simple refers to the division of the beat and relates to the bottom figure in the signature, while the term binary refers to the division of the measure and relates to the top figure in the signature.

The meters used in this unit are listed here for reference.

Simple Binary Meter

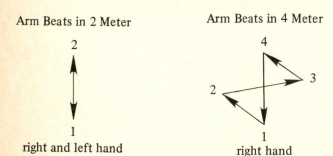

ARM BEATS

One way to physically demonstrate as well as experience a given metric design is to use gestures known as arm beats. As a given tempo quickens, the time between beats must shrink. Therefore, the arm-beat pattern must be reduced in size, and consequently the amount of energy consumed for the execution of the pattern must be decreased. Likewise, as a given tempo slackens, the time between beats must lengthen and, therefore, the arm-beat pattern must be enlarged; consequently, the amount of energy consumed for the execution of the pattern must be increased.

Arm Beats in 2 Meter   Arm Beats in 4 Meter

right and left hand   right hand

note: when using two arms, one arm is the mirror image of the other.

The execution of the arm-beat patterns should reflect every quality of the music: tempo, dynamics, articulation, etc., as well as mark the beat in time and space. For this reason the arm beats are a vital tool for helping the sight reader gain fluency and proficiency. Therefore, all remaining exercises contained in this volume should be practiced and performed with the appropriate arm-beat pattern.

RHYTHM

Thus far, the concepts of beat and meter have been defined without any reference to the concept of rhythm. However, beats and meters are components inherent in the rhythm of Western music. Without rhythm, neither concept of beat nor meter would have reason to exist. Therefore, rhythm is an organized series of sounds and silences of various lengths that travel through space, in time and with energy. The organization of these sounds and silences determine what is known as the *beat,* which recurs and forms the structure known as meter. See examples 1, 2, and 3.

In example 1, the rhythm of the entire piece is made up of sounds of one duration that happens to match the beat note value. However, in example 2, the rhythm of the composition is made up of sounds and silences. Even though the sounds and silences match the beat–note value, the rhythm is far more interesting. The use of silence [♪] gives perspective to sound and invites one to listen. Furthermore, in example 3, the rhythm of the piece is composed of sounds and silences of various duration. With this added dimension, music composition can create an infinite variety of images. The rhythmic durations used here are:

[𝅝] the whole note	[𝄻] the whole rest
[𝅗𝅥] the half note	[𝄼] the half rest
[♩] the quarter note	[𝄽] the quarter rest
[♪] the eighth note	[𝄾] the eighth rest
[𝅘𝅥𝅯] the sixteenth note	[𝄿] the sixteenth rest

The following chart illustrates the metric and spacial relationship among the various durations.

* The upper-note value is the *multiple* of the lower-note value.

† The lower-note value is the *division* of the upper-note value.

PATTERN

By organizing the various durations into measures, rhythmic pattern is created. The following patterns are employed in this unit. Notice that each note value is alloted a portion of space in direct relation to its duration. For example, if a half note [𝅗𝅥] takes the same amount of time as two quarter notes [♩♩], then it follows that the half note must take up the same portion of space as two quarter notes [𝅗𝅥 ♩].

While studying the following chart, make special note of the patterns marked by an asterisk (*). [These patterns contain more than one type of note value and have names given to them by the ancient Greeks.] Patterns *d* and *i* are *anapest* [′an·ə·pest] (short, short, long). Patterns *e* and *j* are *dactylic* [′dak·til·ik] (long, short, short).

PATTERNS FOR STUDY
simple binary (or duple) meter

2 Meter	(a)
	(b)
	(c)
	(d)*
	(e)*
4 Meter	(f)
	(g)
	(h)
	(i)*
	(j)*

SIMPLE TERNARY (OR TRIPLE) METER

ARM BEATS

This unit is also concerned with a simple meter in 3. Any meter having three beats is referred to as a ternary, or triple, meter. Obviously, the ternary meter contains three stress types: *crusic, preanacrusic metacrusic,* and *anacrusic,* in that order.

Arm Beats in 3 Meter

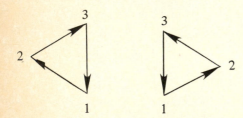

NOTE VALUES

The new note values introduced in this unit are the dotted half note [♩.], the dotted quarter note [♩.], and the dotted eighth note [♪.]. The spacial relationship between these note values and their multiples is illustrated below.

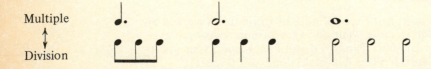

PATTERNS IN 3 METER

The following patterns in 3 meter are employed in this unit. Take note of patterns *c* and *d*. Pattern *c* is known as *trochaic* [trō·ˈkā·ik] (long, short). The rhythm is often pronounced in French [ˈtro·chā], since the pronounciation fits exactly with the rhythm of the pattern. Pattern *d* is known as *iambic* [ī·ˈam·bik] (short, long). This pattern is pronounced as well in the French [ˈē·ambe], since it also matches the rhythm of the pattern.

PATTERNS FOR STUDY
simple ternary (or triple) meter

PITCH: *Major and Minor Thirds*

The interval size of the *third* spans three different pitch names. The minor third (m3) consists of three half steps and the major third (M3) consists of four half steps (or two whole steps). Thirds are among the most common intervals and are used as the building blocks of most of the chords in tonal music.

In the following illustrations, we can see the various combinations of thirds that exist melodically in the major scale (see example 4) and the chords, or *triads,* which result from building additional thirds onto each scale degree (see example 5).

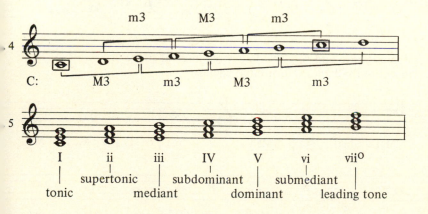

Any triad will consist of a *root* (the lowest note), a *third* (a third above the root), and a *fifth* (a fifth above the root). The four types of triads are major, minor, diminished, and augmented, consisting of the following interval combinations:

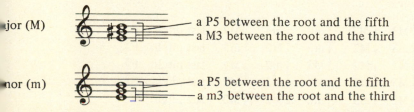

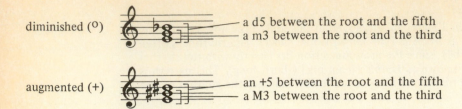

diminished (°) — a d5 between the root and the fifth
— a m3 between the root and the third

augmented (+) — an +5 between the root and the fifth
— a M3 between the root and the third

Before proceeding with the pitch exercises, practice the following patterns, which illustrate where major and minor thirds are found in a tonal framework. Use scale degree numbers and neutral syllables (da, ba, la, etc.).

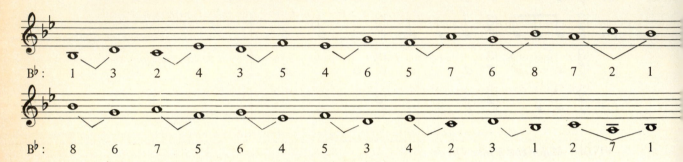

B♭:   1   3   2   4   3   5   4   6   5   7   6   8   7   2   1

B♭:   8   6   7   5   6   4   5   3   4   2   3   1   2   7   1

PITCH EXERCISES
Major and Minor Thirds

1. At the piano, play each note where written, match the pitch in your own vocal range, and sing: a) m3 above, b) M3 above, c) m3 below, and d) M3 below.

2. Play and match each pitch as above and sing the designated interval above or below the given note. Use neutral syllables and/or pitch names.

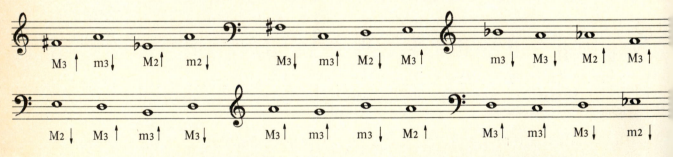

M3↑ m3↓ M2↑ m2↓   M3↓ m3↑ M2↓ M3↑   m3↓ M3↓ M2↑ M3↑

M2↓ M3↑ m3↑ M3↓   M3↑ m3↑ m3↓ M2↑   M3↑ m3↑ M3↓ m2↑

3. Play the given pitch. Then sing the progression of intervals in the direction indicated. You should end up on the given last pitch. Use neutral syllables and pitch names.

a. given pitch: C ↑M3 ↓M2 ↑m2 ↓m3 ↑M2 last pitch: D
b. given pitch: G ↓m3 ↓M2 ↓m2 ↑M2 ↑m3 last pitch: F♯
c. given pitch: A ↓M2 ↓M2 ↑M3 ↓m2 ↓M2 last pitch: F♯
d. given pitch: D♯ ↓M3 ↑m3 ↓M2 ↓m2 ↑M2 last pitch: C♯
e. given pitch: G♯ ↓M2 ↓m3 ↑m2 ↓M2 ↓M2 last pitch: C

4. Sing major, minor, diminished, and augmented triads using the given pitch as:

    a. the root (use the numbers 1 3 5 3 1)

    b. the third (use numbers 3 1 3 5 3)

    c. the fifth (use numbers 5 3 1 3 5)

RHYTHM READING

On each exercise perform the tasks in the order given while using the arm-beat pattern. Use a variety of tempi and dynamics.

1. Articulate the rhythm on neutral syllables (da, ba, la, etc.).

2. Improvise a major melody using a variety of intervals and end on tonic. Use a variety of tonalities.

3. Improvise a major melody using only major and minor seconds and thirds and end on tonic. Use a variety of tonalities.

CLEF READING

On each exercise perform the tasks in the order given while conducting the meter. Use a metronome, beginning at a slow tempo and increasing the rate of speed daily. Invent your own articulation for exercises that are unedited.

1. Speak the rhythm on syllables that will produce the desired articulation.
2. Speak (not sing) the letter name of each note out loud in the designated clefs in proper rhythm while observing the correct articulation.

MELODIES

1. Establish tonic and pulse before beginning. Sing each melody on neutral syllables, scale degree numbers, pitch names, or solfeggio syllables.
2. Use arm beats while singing each melody.
3. Accompany selected melodies with an appropriate harmonization in various styles.

Andante — Sontonga

Fast

Allegro — *Gloucestershire Wassail*

Andante — *Dowland*

Waltz-like

Norwegian Folk Song
Fine

Lively

15.

D.C. al Fine

Allegro

16.

Czechoslovakia

Moderato

17.

DUETS

1. Divide the class in half to perform the duets.
2. Have two students perform the duets.
3. Sing one line and clap the rhythm of the other.
4. Sing one line and perform the other on the piano (play and sing).

1.

RHYTHM: *Changing Meter (Simple)*
PITCH: *Perfect Fourth and Fifth*
CLEFS: *Treble, Bass, and Alto*

RHYTHM: *Changing Meter (Simple)*

Meter as defined in unit 2 is the result of the structuring of beats into a recurring series of stresses known as a measure. Therefore, *changing meter* implies that there is more than one type of stress series occurring within the scope of a single composition. In other words, within a composition containing changing meter, the distance or space from one crusic stress to the next is not consistent.

Two types of changing meter are found in Western music. They are: 1) changing meters where the beat-note value changes (see unit 9), and 2) changing meters where one note value is maintained as the beat note. This last type is the most common means of changing meter and is the simplest. The change in distance from one crusis to another occurs because of a change in the number of beats per measure. The first measure may have two beats; the second, four; the third, three; etc. It should be noted however, that the tempo of the beat note and its divisions remains constant from measure to measure. Therefore, the relationship from measure to measure is established and maintained by the beat. This is known as a beat-to-beat relationship [♩ = ♩].

PITCH: *Perfect Fourth and Perfect Fifth*

The significance of the perfect fourth (P4) and the perfect fifth (P5) in tonal music cannot be overstated. The intervals of the P5 between the tonic and dominant and the P4 between the dominant and the upper tonic provide a strong framework for the to-nality. The interval of the fourth spans four different letter names (C D E F) and the fifth, five different letter names (C D E F G). The *perfect* quality of fourths and fifths will usually exist if the sign (natural, sharp, or flat) is the same for both notes in the interval. This can be seen in the following example.

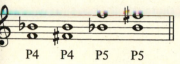

P4 P4 P4   P5 P5 P5

The exception is when the notes b and f are both contained in the interval. In this case, one of the notes will be sharped or flatted.

P4   P4   P5   P5

The identification and singing of perfect fourths and fifths can be aided by thinking of the interval in a tonal context. For example, to reproduce a P5, think the scale degrees 1↑5. To reproduce a P4, think 5↑1.

Before proceeding with the pitch exercises, practice the following patterns, which illustrate how the P4 and P5 function in a tonal framework. Use scale degree numbers and a neutral syllable.

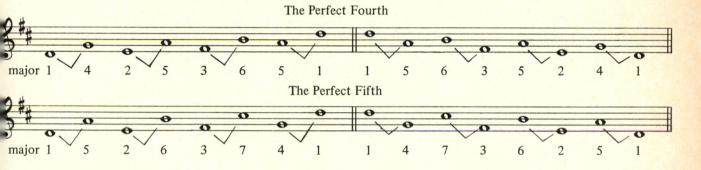

The Perfect Fourth

major 1 4 2 5 3 6 5 1   1 5 6 3 5 2 4 1

The Perfect Fifth

major 1 5 2 6 3 7 4 1   1 4 7 3 6 2 5 1

PITCH EXERCISES

1. At the piano, play each note where written, match the pitch in your own vocal range, and sing a a) P4 above, b) P4 below, c) P5 above, and d) P5 below each given pitch.

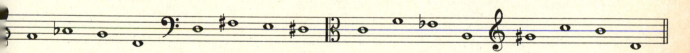

2. Play and match each pitch as above and sing the designated interval above or below the given note. Use a neutral syllable and pitch names.

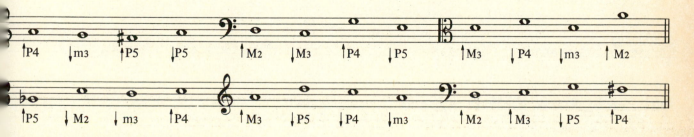

↑P4 ↓m3 ↑P5 ↓P5   ↑M2 ↓M3 ↑P4 ↓P5   ↑M3 ↓P4 ↓m3 ↑M2

↑P5 ↓M2 ↓m3 ↑P4   ↑M3 ↓P5 ↓P4 ↓m3   ↑M2 ↑M3 ↓P5 ↑P4

3. Play the given pitch. Then, using a neutral syllable or pitch names, sing the intervals in the direction indicated. You should end up on the given last pitch.

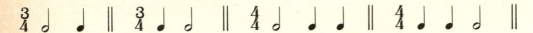

a.   given pitch: C ↑M3 ↓M2 ↑P4 ↓m2 ↓P5   last pitch: B
b.   given pitch: D ↑M3 ↑m3 ↓P4 ↑M3 ↓M2   last pitch: F♯
c.   given pitch: E♭ ↑P5 ↓m3 ↑m2 ↓M2 ↓P4   last pitch: D♭
d.   given pitch: F♯ ↓P4 ↑m2 ↑P4 ↓M2 ↑P4   last pitch: B♭
e.   given pitch: E ↓m3 ↑P4 ↓P5 ↑m2 ↑M2   last pitch: D

4. Establish the given key by singing the tonic triad on 1 3 5 3 1. Then, sing the given pattern on scale degree numbers.

a.   E major: 1   3   5   6   2   5   1   2   3   5   2   7   1
b.   A major: 8   5   6   4   5   3   1   4   2   6   5   3   1
c.   G major: 1   3   1 ↓ 5 ↑ 2   7   1   3   5   6   4   5   3
d.   D major: 1   3   6   5   8   5   3   4   5   2   3   7   1
e.   A major: 3   4   5   8   6   4   5 ↑ 2   1   3 ↓ 6   7   8

Perform the above using the following rhythmic patterns. Use a neutral syllable or pitch names.

PITCH PATTERNS

Play the tonic pitch and establish tonic by singing 1 3 5 3 1. Then, sing the pitch patterns on a neutral syllable, numbers, pitch names, or solfeggio syllables.

Each unit will now contain some pitch patterns without key signatures. Determine the tonality before proceeding as above.

RHYTHM READING I

On each exercise perform the tasks in the order given while using arm-beat patterns. Use a variety of tempi and dynamics. Improvise rhythm in all blank measures.

1. Articulate the rhythm on neutral syllables (da, ba, la, etc.).

2. Improvise a major melody using a variety of intervals and end on tonic. Use a variety of tonalities.

3. Improvise a major melody using intervals no larger than a perfect fifth and end on tonic. Use a variety of tonalities.

RHYTHM READING II

On each exercise perform the tasks in the order given. Use a variety of tempi and dynamics. Invent rhythm in all blank spaces.

1. Articulate the rhythm of each voice on neutral syllables (da, ba, la, etc.) while employing the arm-beat patterns.

2. Improvise a major melody on each voice using a variety of intervals and ending on tonic while employing the arm-beat patterns.

3. Improvise a major melody on the soprano voice using a variety of intervals while clapping the rhythm of the bottom voice. End on tonic.

CLEF READING

On each exercise, perform the tasks in the order given while using the arm–beat patterns. Use a metronome, beginning at a slow tempo and increasing the rate of speed daily. Invent your own articulation for those exercises that are unedited.

1. Speak the rhythm on syllables that will produce the desired articulation.
2. Speak (not sing) the letter name of each note out loud in the designated clefs while observing the correct articulation.

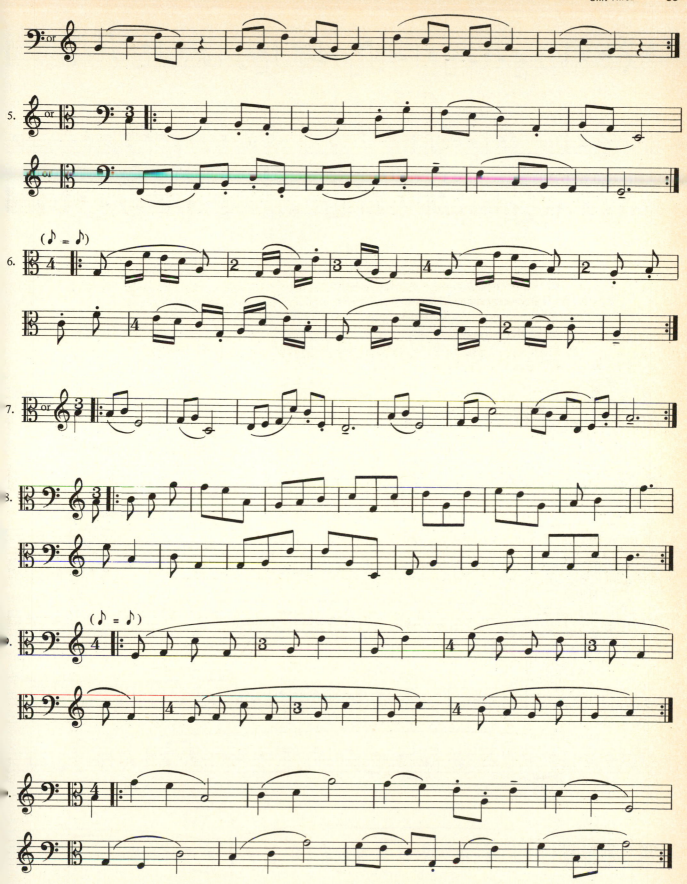

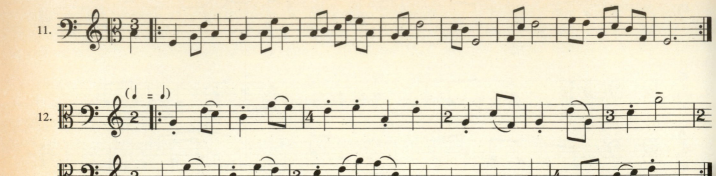

MELODIES

1. Establish tonic and pulse before beginning. Sing each melody on a neutral syllable, scale degree numbers, pitch names, or solfeggio syllables.

2. Use arm-beat patterns while singing each melody.

3. Accompany selected melodies (teacher in class or student while practicing) with an appropriate harmonization in various styles.

4. Before performing the alto clef melodies, read the pitch names in the proper rhythm, then sing.

Chanson bocagère

18.

Slavonic Folk Song

19.

Polish Folk Song

20.

Chanson

21.

22. Allegro   Lully
     mf

23. Lively   *Iceland*
     mp
     mf

24. Allegretto   Rathgeber
     mf
     mp
     mf

25. Andante   *German Folk Song*
     mp
     p

Lup

26. Andante

DUETS

1. Divide the class in half to perform the duets.
2. Have two students perform the duets.
3. Sing one line and clap the rhythm of the other.
4. Sing one line and perform the other on the piano (play and sing).

1. Allegro   *Anonymous*

Andante

Niccolò dá Perugia

Praetorius

RHYTHM: *Compound Meter (Duple, Triple, and Quadruple)*
PITCH: *Major and Minor Sixths; Major and Minor Sevenths*
CLEFS: *Treble, Bass, and Alto*

RHYTHM: *Compound Meter (Duple, Triple, and Quadruple)*

When listening to and performing music, it is clear that there is a distinct physical difference between the experience of compound meter and that of simple meter. One way to describe the difference is to say that compound meter gives one a physical sensation of circular motion, while simple meter gives one a physical sensation of angular motion. The reason for this corporal difference lies in the use of beat-note values and the manner in which these beat-notes are divided. Simple meters employ beat-note values that are divisible by two while compound meters employ beat-note values that are divisible by three. The typical beat-note values in compound meter are the dotted quarter note [♩.], the dotted eighth note [♪.], and the dotted half note [𝅗𝅥.].

It would follow that the typical meter signatures employing compound division should be notated in like manner: ²⁄♩. , ²⁄♪. , ³⁄♩. , ³⁄♪. , ⁴⁄♩. , ⁴⁄♪. . However, the traditional method of notating compound meters is to notate the number of divisions in a measure and the value of each division rather than notating beats. The following diagram will serve to illustrate.

compound duple

compound triple

compound quadruple

In theory, the arm–beat patterns for compound meters are identical to those for simple meters. However, such is not the case in practice. When performing the arm–beat patterns in compound meter, a definite circular or curved motion is employed while traveling to and from each beat. This is in contrast to the rather straight and angular motion employed while performing simple meter patterns.

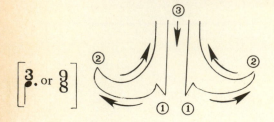

The rhythmic patterns employed in this unit have, in a sense, already been studied in unit 2, where each rhythmic pattern encompasses an entire measure: [♩.], [♪♪♪], [♪♪], [♪♪]. However, in this unit, these same patterns are reduced or diminished to encompass one dotted beat note.

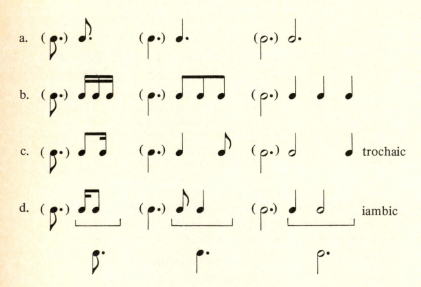

c. trochaic

d. iambic

PITCH: *Major and Minor Sixth*

The interval of the sixth encompasses six different note names (C D E F G A). The major sixth (M6) occurs between the scale degrees 1↕6, 2↕7, 4↕2, and 5↕3. Minor sixths (m6) occur between the scale degrees 3↕1 and 6↕4. When writing and singing minor sixths, it is helpful to think of the distance between the notes as a P5 plus a m2. A major sixth can be thought of as a P5 plus a M2.

Before proceeding with the pitch exercises, practice sixths in the following ways:

1. Spell and sing major and minor sixths as described below using a neutral syllable and pitch names. Begin on many different pitches.

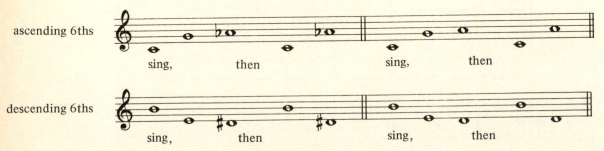

ascending 6ths

sing,   then   sing,   then

descending 6ths

sing,   then   sing,   then

2. Practice the following pattern, which illustrates where major and minor sixths are found in a tonal framework. Use scale degree numbers and a neutral syllable.

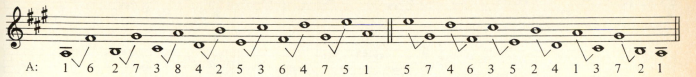

A: 1   6   2   7   3   8   4   2   5   3   6   4   7   5   1   5   7   4   6   3   5   2   4   1   3   7   2   1

PITCH EXERCISES
Major and Minor Sixths

1. At the piano, play each note where written, match the pitch in your own vocal range, and sing a a) M6 above, b) m6 above, c) M6 below, and d) m6 below each note.

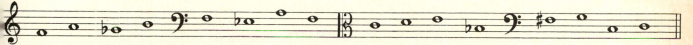

2. Play and match each pitch as above and sing the designated interval above or below the given note. Use a neutral syllable or pitch names.

M6↑   M3↑   m2↓   m6↓   m6↓   M6↑   M2↑   m3↓   m3↓   P4↑   M3↓   M6↑

P5↑   M6↓   m6↓   m3↓   m6↓   P4↑   M3↓   m2↑   M2↓   P4↓   P5↓   M6↑

3. Play the given pitch and then perform the interval progression using a neutral syllable or pitch names. You should end up on the last pitch.

a.   given pitch: C   ↑M6 ↓M2 ↓m2 ↑P4 ↓M2   last pitch: A
b.   given pitch: F   ↑M3 ↓m6 ↑m2 ↑M2 ↓M3   last pitch: C
c.   given pitch: A♭   ↓m2 ↓M2 ↑m6 ↓m3 ↓m2   last pitch: A
d.   given pitch: A   ↓m6 ↑m2 ↑M2 ↓P5 ↑P4   last pitch: D
e.   given pitch: D   ↑m6 ↓P5 ↑M2 ↓m2 ↑P4   last pitch: A

4. Establish the tonality by singing the tonic triad. Then perform the pitch patterns using scale degree numbers.

a.   A major: 1   3   5   1↑6   5   8↓3   4   5   1
b.   B major: 3   4   5   8↓3   5↓7   1   2   3   4   6   7   8
c.   C major: 5   3   6↓1   2   3   8   4   5↓7   1
d.   E♭ major: 1   3   6   5   8   3   5↓7   1↑6   5   8
e.   B♭ major: 5   3   6   5↑3   2   1↓3   4   5   1

Perform the preceding patterns using the following rhythms. Use a neutral syllable or numbers.

$\frac{3}{3}$ ♩ ♪♩ ♪║ $\frac{6}{8}$ ♪♩ ♪♩║ $\frac{6}{8}$ ♪♪♪♩.║ $\frac{6}{8}$ ♩ ♪♪♪║

PITCH PATTERNS: *Major and Minor Sixths*

Play the tonic pitch and establish tonic by singing 1 3 5 3 1. Then sing the pitch patterns on a neutral syllable, scale degree numbers, or pitch names.

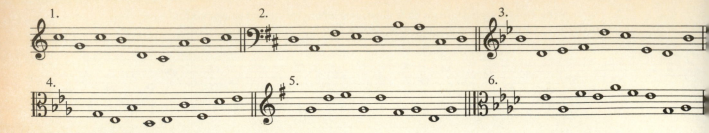

Determine the tonality before proceeding as above.

Melodies using major and minor sixths can be found on page 53.

PITCH: *Major and Minor Seventh*

The interval of the seventh encompasses seven different pitch names (for example,

C D E F G A B). As the seventh is closest in size to the octave, it can easily be spelled and vocally reproduced by relating it aurally and visually to the octave. A major seventh (M7) can be thought of as a perfect octave (P8) minus a m2, and a minor seventh (m7) can be thought of as a P8 minus a M2. Before proceeding with the pitch exercises, practice sevenths in the following ways:

1. Sing sevenths as indicated below. Use a neutral syllable and pitch names. Begin on many different pitches.

2. Practice the following pattern, which illustrates where major and minor sevenths are found in a tonal framework. Use scale degree numbers and a neutral syllable.

PITCH EXERCISES
Major and Minor Sevenths

1. At the piano, play each note where written, match the pitch in your own vocal range and sing a a) M7 above, b) m7 above, c) M7 below, and d) m7 below each note.

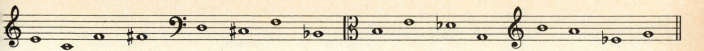

2. Play and match each pitch as above and sing the designated interval above or below the given note. Use a neutral syllable or pitch names.

3. Play the given pitch and then perform the interval progression using a neutral syllable and pitch names. You should end up on the last pitch.

a. given pitch: D ↑M7 ↑m2 ↓P5 ↑M2 ↓m7 last pitch: B
b. given pitch: E ↑M3 ↓m7 ↑m2 ↑P4 ↑m3 last pitch: G
c. given pitch: B ↑m3 ↓m2 ↑m7 ↑M2 ↓M3 last pitch: F
d. given pitch: F♯ ↑M2 ↑M2 ↑m3 ↓M7 ↑m2 last pitch: E♭
e. given pitch: G ↓m2 ↑M3 ↓P5 ↑m6 ↓M7 last pitch: C

4. Establish your tonality by singing the tonic triad. Then, perform the pitch patterns using scale degree numbers.

a. G major: 3 2 1↓ 5↑4 3 2↑5 ↓6 7 1
b. B♭ major: 8 5 8↓ 2 3 4 5 6↓7 2 1
c. C major: 1 7 8 5 3 6↓ 7 1 3 2 1
d. E♭ major: 5↓6 7 1 2 3 6 5↓5↑4 2 1
e. G major: 1 5 6↓7↑5↓6↑4↓5↑3↓4↑2 7 1

Perform the preceding patterns using the following rhythms. Use a neutral syllable or numbers.

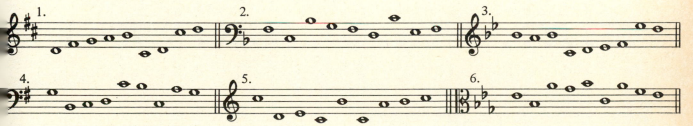

PITCH PATTERNS: *Major and Minor Sevenths*

Play the tonic pitch and establish tonic by singing the tonic triad. Then sing the pitch patterns on a neutral syllable, scale degree numbers, pitch names, or solfeggio syllables.

Determine the tonality before proceeding as above.

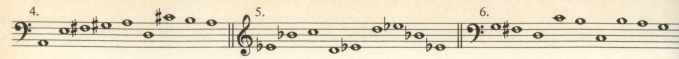

Melodies using major and minor sevenths can be found on page 57.

RHYTHM READING I

On each exercise perform the tasks in the order given while conducting the meter.
Use a variety of tempi and dynamics. Invent rhythms in all blank measures.

1. Articulate the rhythm of neutral syllables (da, ba, la, etc.)
2. Improvise a major melody using a variety of intervals and end on tonic. Use a variety of tonalities.
3. Improvise a major melody using intervals no larger than a major sixth and end on tonic. Use a variety of tonalities.

RHYTHM READING II

On each exercise perform the tasks in the order given. Use a variety of tempi and dynamics. Invent rhythm in all blank measures.

1. Articulate the rhythm of each voice on neutral syllables while conducting the meter.
2. Improvise a major melody on each voice using a variety of intervals while conducting the meter. End on tonic.
3. Improvise a major melody on the soprano voice using a variety of intervals while clapping the rhythm of the bottom voice. End on tonic.

CLEF READING

On each exercise perform the tasks in the order given while conducting the meter. Employ the metronome, beginning at a slow tempo and increasing the rate of speed daily. Invent your own articulation for unedited exercises.

1. Speak the rhythm on syllables that will best produce the desired articulation.
2. Speak (not sing) the letter name of each note out loud in the designated clef while observing the correct articulation.

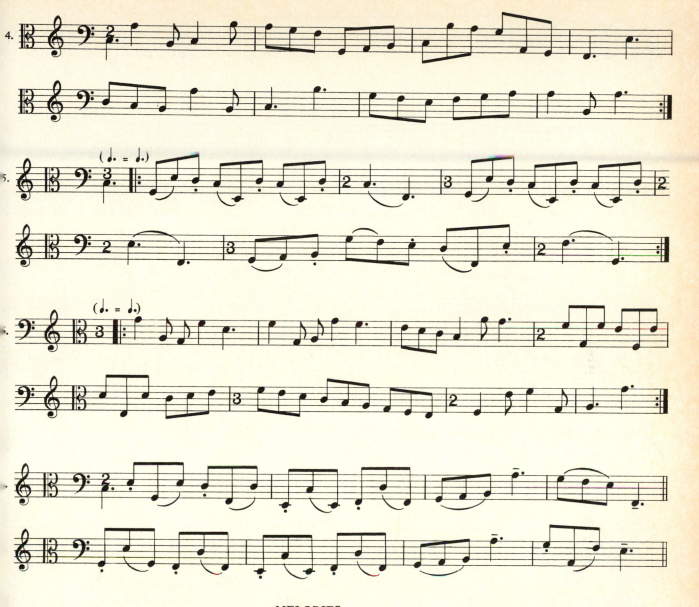

MELODIES

1. Establish tonic and pulse. Sing each melody on a neutral syllable, scale degree numbers or pitch names.
2. Accompany selected melodies with an appropriate harmonization in various styles.
3. Use arm-beat patterns while singing each melody.
4. Before performing alto clef melodies, read the pitch names in the proper rhythm, then sing.

Major and Minor Sixths

Mozart

Allegretto

2.

Rutter

Allegretto

3.

Andante

4.

Briskly

Spai

5.

Lebhaft

Brahms

Major and Minor Sevenths

Andante

Anonymous

1.

Presto

Kücken

Old English Air

Gracefully

Allegro
Rochlitz
8.

Andante
Dalcroze

Langsam
Böhm

Adagio

DUETS

1. Divide the class in half to perform duets.
2. Have two students sing the duets.
3. Sing one line and clap the rhythm of the other.
4. Sing one line and perform the other on the piano (play and sing).

Je port amiablement

Donato da Firenze

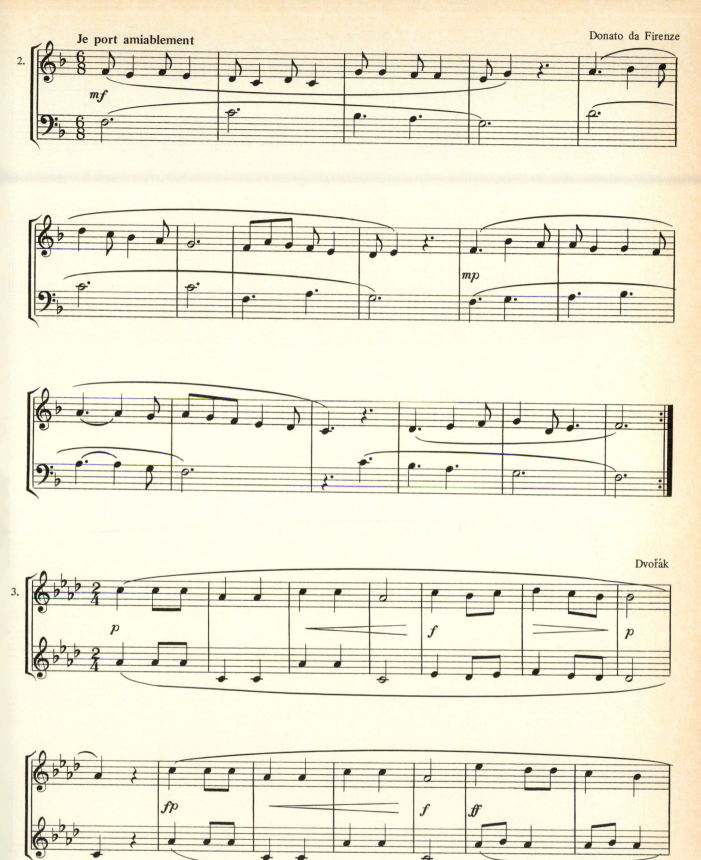

Dvořák

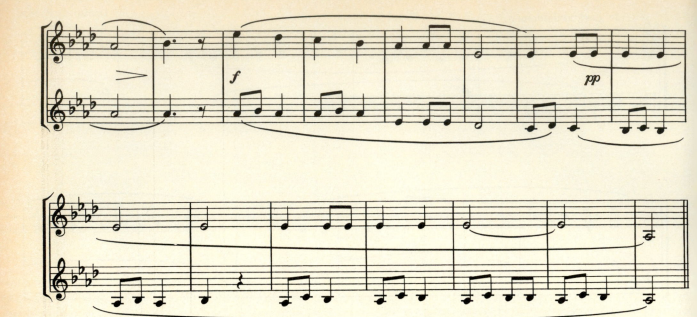

RHYTHM: *Complementary Rhythm*
PITCH: *Tritone*
CLEFS: *Treble, Bass, and Alto*

RHYTHM: *Complementary Rhythm*

Complementary rhythm is the underlying, independent rhythmic phrase derived from an original phrase. The original phrase is called the *pattern*, and the underlying phrase is referred to as the *complement*. The complement may use a combination of any note values or employ the exclusive use of one note value. The only regulation is that the complementary rhythm not initiate sound at those points in time and space where the pattern has already done so. The following examples are offered for analysis. Note that the pattern may contain note values and/or silences of any duration.

ex. 1: complement at the quarter note

pattern
complement

x. 2: complement at the eighth note

pattern
complement

x. 3: complement at the sixteenth note

pattern
complement

etc.

. 4: complement at the half note

pattern
complement

ex. 5: mixed complement

pattern
complement

PITCH: *Tritone*

The *tritone* derives its name from the fact that it consists of three whole steps. Within the major scale, it exists between the fourth and seventh scale degrees and is known specifically as an augmented fourth (+4) or diminished fifth (^{o}5). It is one of the most unstable intervals in tonal music and therefore must resolve. The ^{o}5 normally resolves inward to a third and the +4 normally resolves outward to a sixth.

C: 4 - - - -3   7 - - - - 1
      7 - - - -1   4 - - - - 3

When the interval of the tritone is found melodically, the last note occuring will generally be the one to resolve, the fourth scale degree resolving down to three or the seventh scale degree resolving up to one.

When spelling tritones, it is helpful to relate the interval to its perfect counterpart. That is, an +4 can be thought of as a P4 plus a half step and a ^{o}5 can be thought of as a P5 minus a half step. In both cases, the pitch names will remain the same.

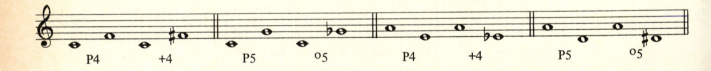

P4   +4   P5 ^{o}5   P4   +4   P5 ^{o}5

When singing the interval of the tritone out of a tonal context, it is helpful to first sing a P4, add a half step, and then sing the tritone alone. Practice singing tritones as illustrated below before proceeding with the pitch exercises.

sing,   then   sing,   then

PITCH EXERCISES
Tritone

1. At the piano, play each note where written, match the pitch in your own vocal range, and sing tritones above and below each pitch.

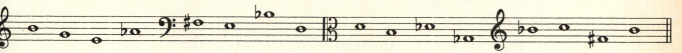

2. Play and match each pitch as above and sing the designated interval above or below the given pitch. Use a neutral syllable and pitch names.

3. Play the given pitch. Then, using neutral syllables or pitch names, sing the progression of intervals in the directions indicated. You should end up on the last pitch.

given pitch: A	↓P4	↑+4	↑m2	↓M3	↑M2	last pitch: A
given pitch: G	↑P4	↓°5	↑m2	↓m6	↑m2	last pitch: C
given pitch: D	↑m2	↓M2	↑+4	↑m2	↓M2	last pitch: G♭
given pitch: E♭	↓m3	↑M7	↑m2	↓°5	↑m2	last pitch: G
given pitch: E	↓M3	↓m2	↑°5	↓M2	↑P5	last pitch: B♭

PITCH PATTERNS

Play the tonic pitch and establish tonic by singing 1 3 5 3 1. Then sing the pitch patterns on neutral syllables, scale degree numbers, pitch names, or solfeggio syllables.

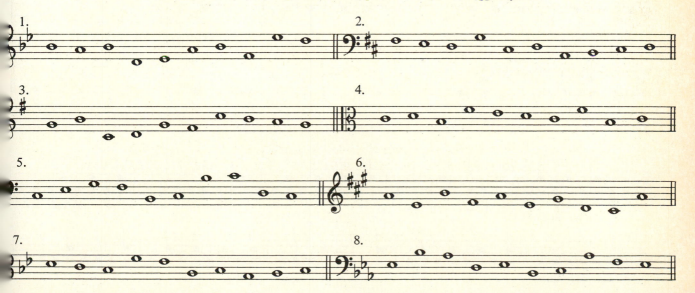

Determine the tonality before proceeding as above.

RHYTHM READING

On each exercise perform the tasks in the order given. Use a variety of tempi and dynamics.

1. Articulate the rhythm of the upper voice (pattern) and then the bottom voice (complement) on neutral syllables while conducting the meter.
2. Articulate the rhythm of the upper voice while tapping the rhythm of the bottom voice.
3. Improvise a major melody on the rhythm of the upper voice using any intervals while using the arm-beat pattern.
4. Improvise a major melody on the rhythm of the upper voice using any intervals while tapping the rhythm of the bottom voice.

(improvise your own complement)

CLEF READING

On each exercise perform the tasks in the order given. Use a metronome, beginning at a slow tempo and increasing the rate of speed daily. Invent your own articulation for exercises that are unedited.

1. Speak the rhythm of the upper voice (pattern) and then the lower voice (complement) on syllables that produce the desired articulation while using the arm-beat pattern.
2. Speak the rhythm of the upper voice (pattern) on syllables that produce the desired articulation while clapping the rhythm of the lower voice (complement).
3. Speak (not sing) the letter name of each note in the pattern out loud using the designated clefs in proper rhythm while observing the correct articulation and using the arm-beat pattern.
4. Speak (not sing) the letter name of each note in the pattern out loud using the designated clefs in proper rhythm while observing the correct articulation and clapping the complement.
5. Rework each exercise by improvising your own complementary rhythm.

(improvise your own complement)

MELODIES

1. Establish tonic and pulse before beginning. Sing each melody on neutral syllables, scale degree numbers, or pitch names.
2. Use arm-beat patterns while singing each melody.
3. Accompany selected melodies with an appropriate harmonization in various styles.
4. Keeping a given division as a constant, clap a complementary rhythm to the melodies (see possible rhythmic complements to melodies 2 and 4).
5. Before performing the alto clef melodies, read the pitch names in the proper rhythm first, then sing.

Allegro   Mozart

2. Lively   *Czech Folk Song*

3. Moderato

4. Lively   *Hispanic Folk Song*

5. Allegro   *Chaminade*

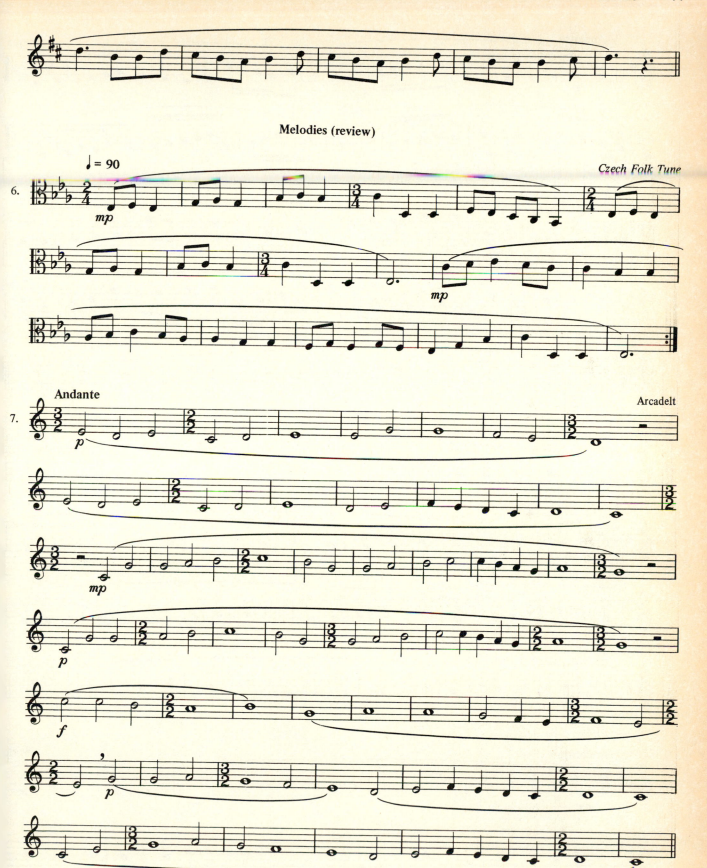

Melodies (review)

6. ♩ = 90

Czech Folk Tune

Andante

Arcadelt

7.

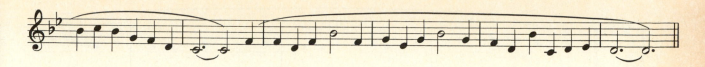

Vivace — Telemann

12.

Andante sostenuto — Puccini

13.

DUETS

1. Divide the class in half to perform duets.
2. Have two students perform the duets.
3. Sing one line and clap the rhythm of the other.
4. Sing one line and perform the other on the piano (play and sing).

Andante — *Anonymous*

1.

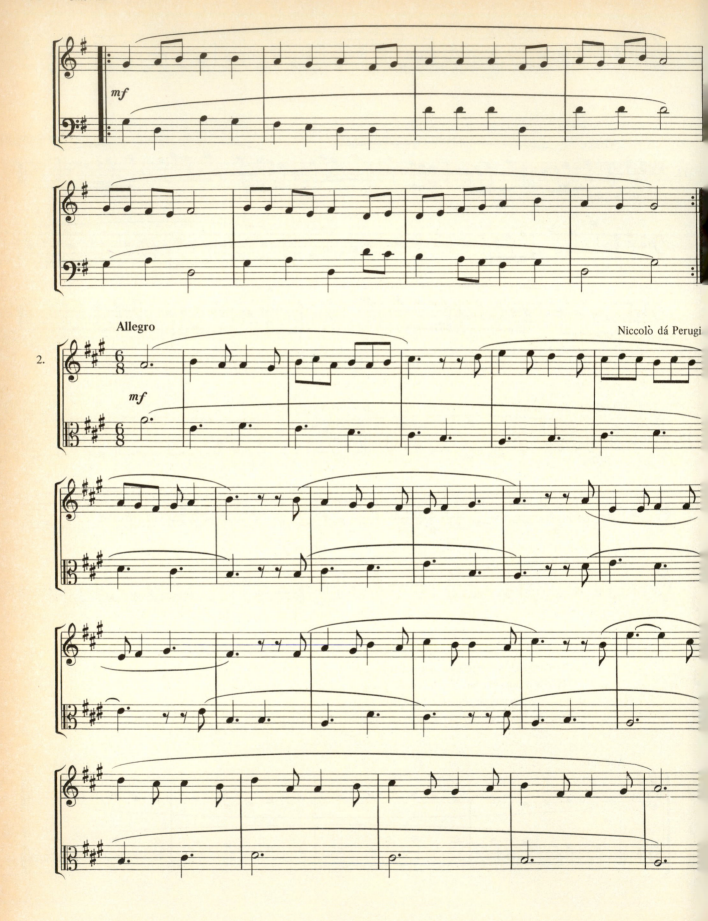

Allegro

Niccolò dá Perugi

RHYTHM: *Syncopation (Within the Measure)*
PITCH: *Minor Mode; Continuation of the Major Mode*
CLEFS: *Treble, Bass, Alto, and Changing Clef*

RHYTHM: *Syncopation (Within the Measure)*

Syncopation is the result of a dramatic conflict between a persistent metric structure and a rhythm pattern striving to resist the predictability of the meter, thereby creating crusic, metacrusic, and anacrusic stresses that sound displaced in time. This sound displacement, however, is not merely an execution of "off-beat" rhythm notation such as countertime and complementary rhythm. Syncopation is a use of a style in the performance of the "off-beat" notation whereby the performing musician creates an illusion of the rhythm being ripped away from the meter and a struggle to maintain this rupture.

In this unit, syncopation patterns are limited to beats within the bar lines. There are two types: syncopation by *retardation* and syncopation by *anticipation*.

Retarded syncopation occurs when a sound is created on the crusis of a given beat and is suspended by use of a tie or augmentation dot beyond the crusis of the next beat.

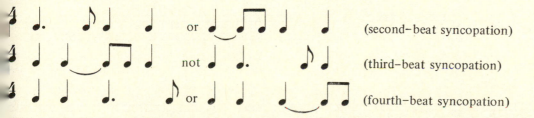

Anticipated syncopation occurs when a sound that would normally occur on the crusis of the next beat is performed earlier and then is suspended by use of a tie or augmentation dot beyond the crusis of the next beat.

Through the study of syncopation one begins to hear and see new rhythmic patterns emerge:

[♩. ♪] or [♩ ♫], binary trochaic; [♪ ♩.   ] or [♫ ♩   ], binary iambic

[♪ ♩ ♩] or [♫ ♫], amphibrach [am·f·brak].

Amphibrach is a most interesting pattern because it is a composite of retarded syncopation [♩.   ♪] and anticipated syncopation [♪ ♩.   ]:

[♩. ♪]
[♪ ♩] played together they sound [♪ ♩ ♪].

PITCH: *Minor Mode*

In units 6 through 9, melodies and exercises will be added that utilize the minor mode. That is, they will be based on notes contained in the minor scale.

There are three different forms of minor scales: natural minor (pure or aeolian), harmonic minor, and melodic minor. The natural minor has no added chromatic alterations. Like the major scale, it is made up of whole and half steps, but in a different sequence. As can be seen below, the half steps in the aeolian scale fall between scale degrees 2–3 and 5–6 as compared to 3–4 and 7–8 in the major scale.

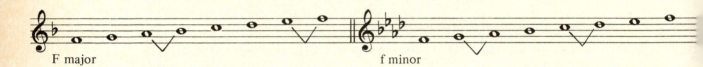

F major   f minor

The harmonic and melodic minor scales are variants of the aeolian scale. The first five notes of the three scales are the same. It is the sixth and seventh scale degrees which differentiate them.

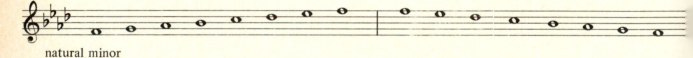

natural minor

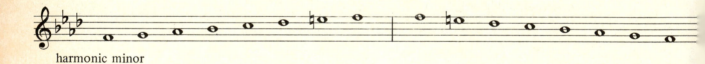

harmonic minor

melodic minor

Note that all three scales have the same key signature. The harmonic minor scale is like the aeolian but has its seventh scale degree raised both in its ascending and descending forms. The melodic minor scale raises the sixth and seventh scale degree in the ascending form but reverts to the natural (aeolian) form when descending. In actual music, the use of the melodic minor scale is often inconsistent. Generally, when the melodic material is ascending, the raised form is used, and when the melodic material is descending, the lowered or natural form is used. This is not always the case, however, as can be seen in melody 18 in this unit and melody 24 in unit 8.

Before proceeding with the pitch exercises, practice by singing scales in the following way:

1. Establish a minor tonic by singing 1 3 5 3 1.
2. Sing an aeolian scale, followed by harmonic and melodic minor scales using the same tonic.

Using numbers when performing these scales can help to identify the scale degrees to be altered. When a familiarity with the sounds of the scales is attained, however, singing on a neutral syllable or pitch names is encouraged.

PITCH EXERCISES

1. Sing minor triads, using the given pitch as:
   a. the root of a minor triad (use the numbers 1 3 5 3 1).
   b. the third of a minor triad (use the numbers 3 1 3 5 3).
   c. the fifth of a minor triad (use the numbers 5 3 1 3 5).

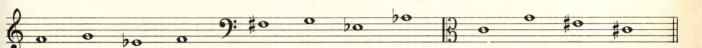

2. Play and match each pitch. Then sing the designated interval above or below the given note. Use a neutral syllable and pitch names.

3. Sing ascending and descending minor scales (natural, harmonic, and melodic) using the following syncopated rhythms. Conduct and use scale degree numbers and a neutral syllable.

4. Establish each tonality. Then perform each pattern in natural, harmonic, and melodic minor. Use scale degree numbers.
   a. c minor: 1 3 5 8↓ 3 4 5↓ 7 1 2 1
   b. a minor: 8 7 8 7 6 5 3 4 5 3 1 7 1
   c. g♯ minor: 1 2 3 1↓ 5 6 7 8↑ 5 3 1↓ 6 5 5 1
   d. e minor: 5 3 4 2 1↑ 7 6 7 8 5 3 4 5↓ 7 1
   e. a♭ minor: 8 5 8 7 6 5 6 7 8↓ 3 4 5 3 1

PITCH PATTERNS

Determine the correct form of minor before performing each pattern.

Play the tonic pitch and establish tonic by singing 1 3 5 3 1. Then sing the patterns on a neutral syllable, scale degree numbers, pitch names, or solfeggio syllables.

Determine the tonality before proceeding as above.

RHYTHM READING

On each exercise perform the tasks in the order given while conducting the meter. Use a variety of tempi and dynamics. Invent rhythms in all blank measures.

1. Articulate the rhythm on neutral syllables (da, ba, la, etc.).

2. Improvise a major melody, then a minor melody, using a variety of intervals, ending on tonic. Use a variety of tonalities.

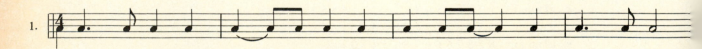

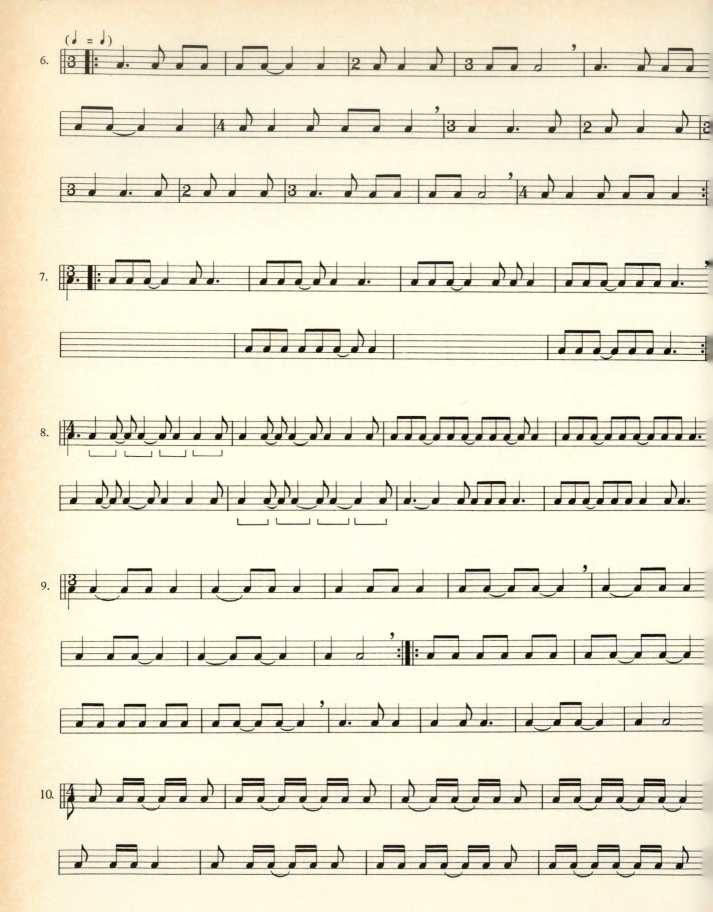

CLEF READING

On each exercise perform the tasks in the order given while using arm-beat patterns. Use a metronome, beginning at a slow tempo and increasing the rate of speed daily. Invent your own articulation for exercises that are unedited.

1. Speak the rhythm on syllables that will produce the desired articulation.
2. Speak (not sing) the letter name of each note out loud in the designated clefs while observing the correct articulation.

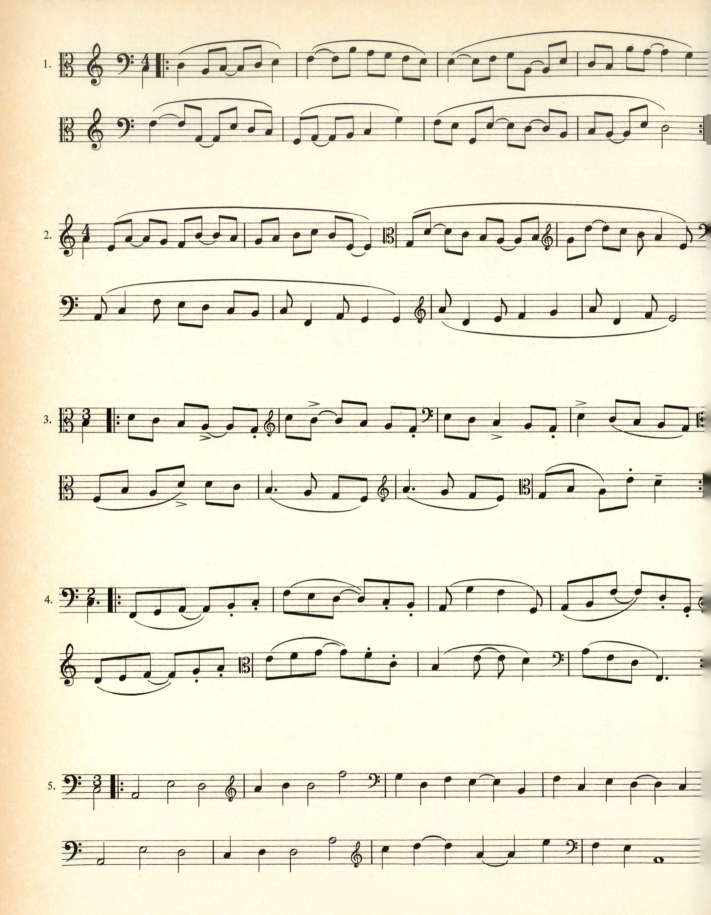

6.

MELODIES

1. Determine the form of minor used in each melody (*note:* additional melodies in the aeolian mode will be found in unit 16).

2. Establish tonic and pulse before beginning. Sing each melody on a neutral syllable, scale degree numbers, pitch names, or solfeggio syllables.

3. Use arm-beat patterns while singing each melody.

4. Accompany selected melodies with an appropriate harmonization in various styles.

5. Clap a complementary rhythm for melodies 4, 8, and 10.

6. Before performing the alto clef melodies, read the pitch names in the proper rhythm, then sing.

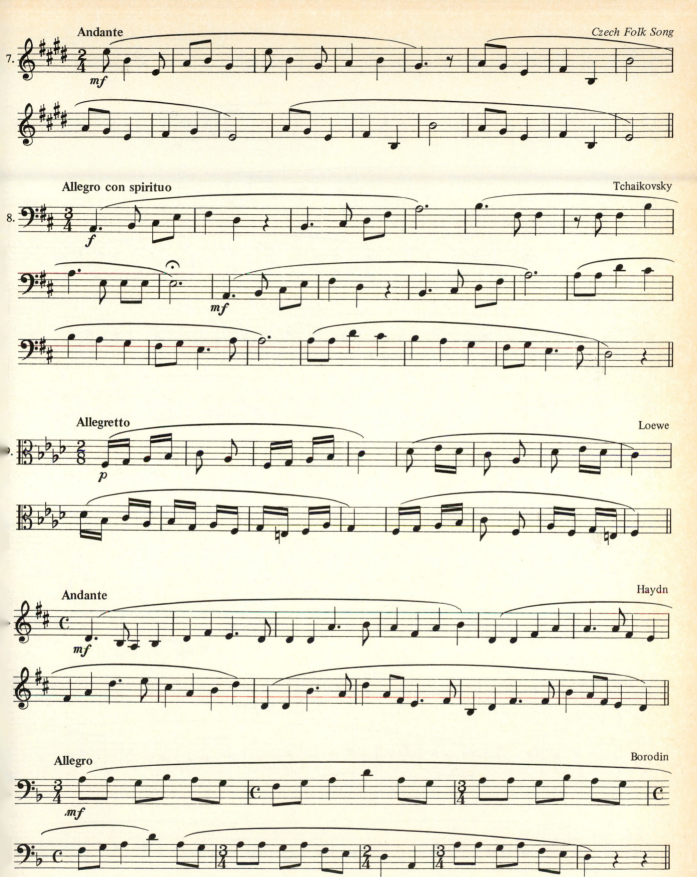

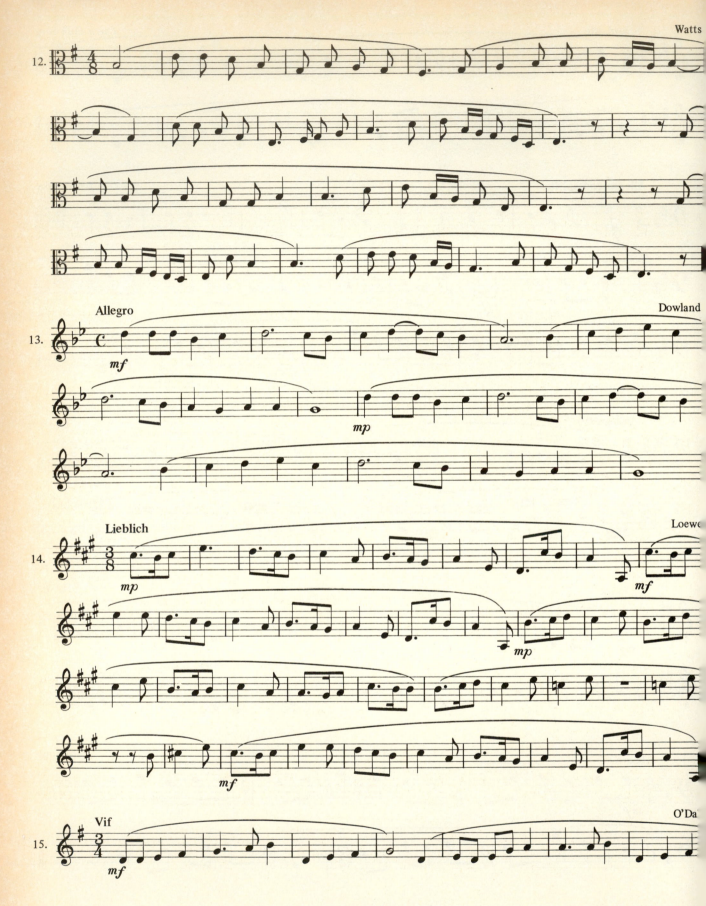

Day

Ruhig

25.

Beethoven

26. ♩ = 90

Moderately slow

Hippesley

27.

Allegro vivo

Rimsky–Korsakov

28.

29. Allegro — *Spiritual*

30. Andante — *Brunette*

DUETS

1. Divide the class in half to perform duets.
2. Have two students perform duets.
3. Sing one line and clap the rhythm of the other.
4. Sing one line and perform the other on the piano (play and sing).

Allegro — *Anonymous*

RHYTHM: *The Beat (Second Division)*
PITCH: *Minor and Major Modes (Continued)*
CLEFS: *Treble, Bass , Alto, and Changing Clef*

RHYTHM: *The Beat (Second Division)*

Units 1 through 6 have dealt with beats and patterns that have divisions and multiples at a 2:1 ratio in simple metric structure and a 3:1 ratio in compound metric structure.

This unit introduces the second division of the beat. This allows a ratio of 4:1 in simple meter and 6:1 in compound. The following charts have been organized to illustrate all of the new rhythm patterns that may be devised within the existing metric structures. Each pattern should first be experienced separately and then several patterns can be combined to form a phrase or be placed against each other to create a counterpoint. Clapping, articulation, vocal improvisation, and arm-beat patterns should be integrated into the learning experience.

After a theoretical analysis of the patterns, it becomes apparent that each pattern is based on one of the five basic rhythmic modes: anapest, trochaic, dactylic, iambic, or amphabrach.

Patterns at a 4:1 Ratio

Patterns at a 6:1 Ratio

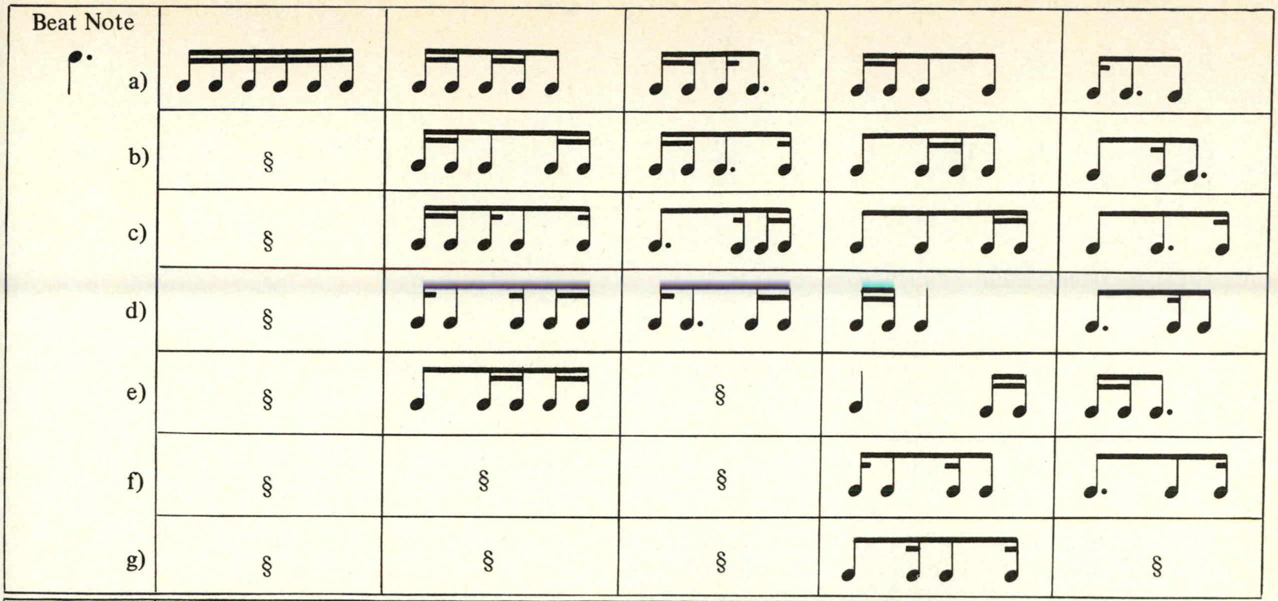

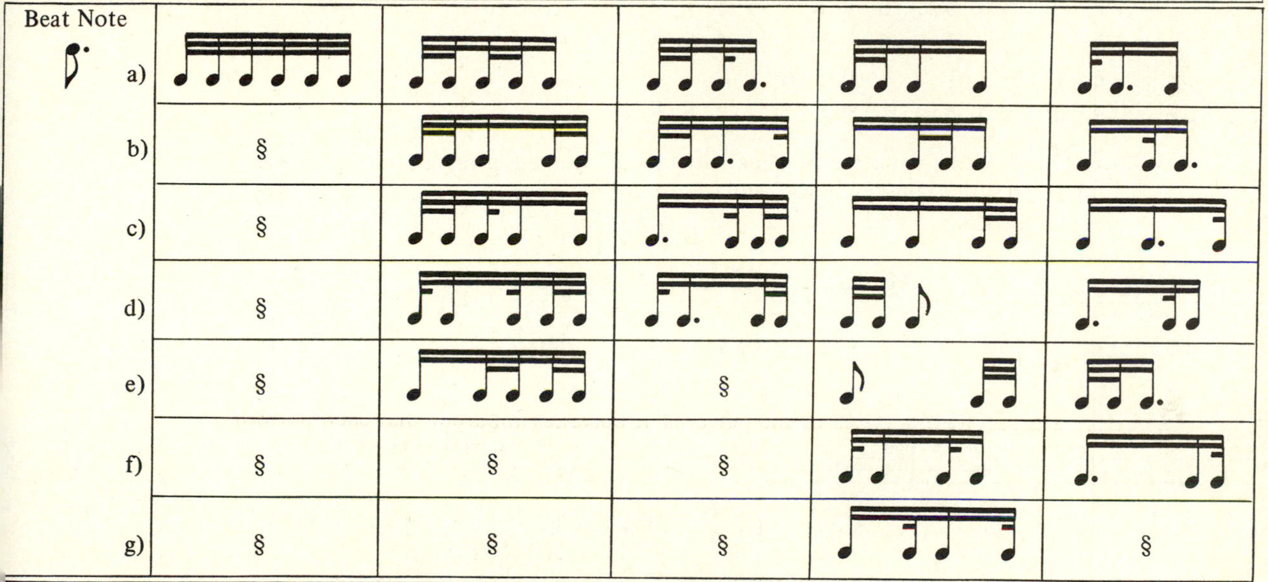

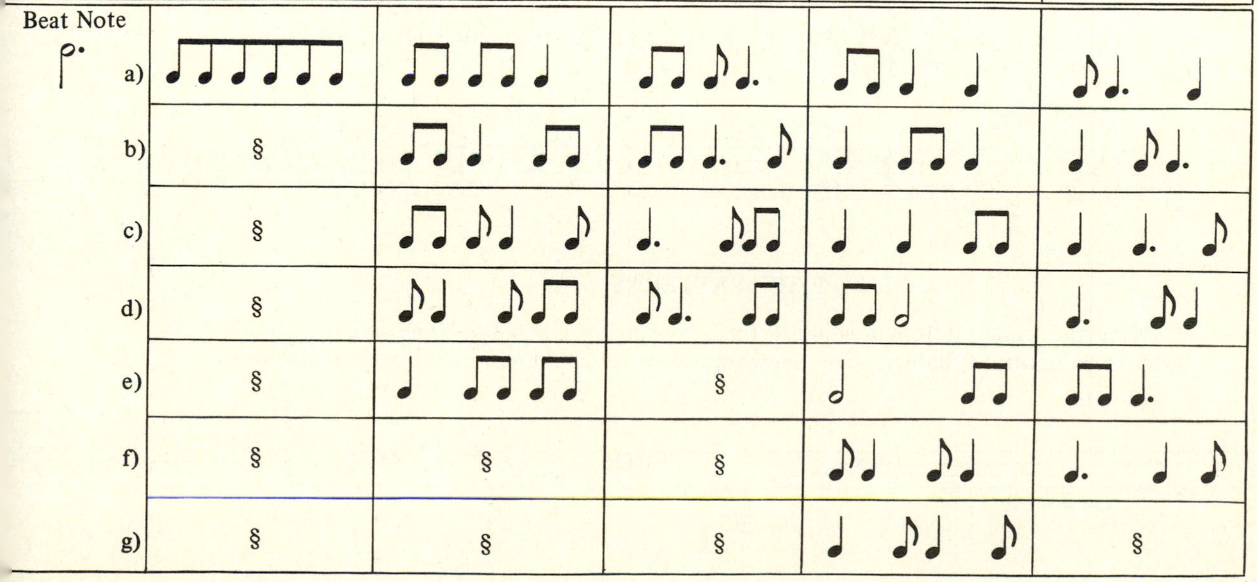

Possible Meter Signatures

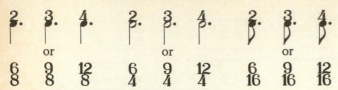

PITCH: *Minor Mode (Continued)*

PITCH EXERCISES

1. Sing the following scales on numbers, neutral syllables, and pitch names (ascending and descending),

   a. c natural minor

   b. d melodic minor

   c. a♭ harmonic minor

   d. e♭ natural minor

   e. b melodic minor

2. Sing the following patterns on scale degree numbers. Sing them first in natural minor, then in harmonic and melodic minor.

   a. c: 1 3 5 3 6 5 8 7 6 5 1

   b. e: 1 7 1 3 5 2 1 5 6 5 7 8

   c. f: 5 3 1 7 1 ↓ 5 6 7 8

   d. d: 3 4 5 1 ↓ 5 ↑ 1 2 3 6 5 8

3. Play and match each pitch. Then, sing the designated interval above or below the given note. Sing on neutral syllables and pitch names.

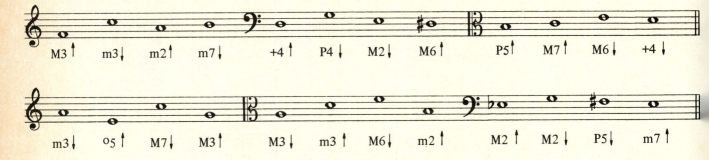

4. Play the given perfect fifths and then sing thirds to create triads. First create major, then minor triads.

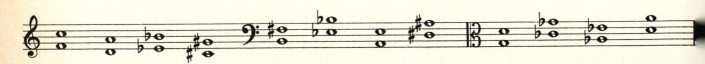

PITCH PATTERNS

Play the tonic pitch and establish tonic by singing 1 3 5 3 1. Then sing the pitch patterns on neutral syllables, scale degree numbers, pitch names, or solfeggio syllables.

Determine the tonality before proceeding as above.

RHYTHM READING I

On each exercise perform the tasks in the order given while using the arm-beat pattern. Use a variety of tempi and dynamics. Invent rhythm in all blank measures.

1. Articulate the rhythm on neutral syllables. (da, ba, la, etc.)

2. Improvise a major melody, then a minor melody, using a variety of intervals, and end on tonic. Use a variety of tonalities.

Additional suggestions:

1. Create your own syncopation exercises by placing ties between beats within the measure.

2. Rewrite several exercises using rhythmic transcription, for example $\frac{6}{8}$ to $\frac{6}{4}$ to $\frac{6}{2}$ and $\frac{4}{4}$ to $\frac{4}{8}$ to $\frac{4}{2}$.

RHYTHM READING II

On each exercise perform the tasks in the order given. Use a variety of tempi and dynamics. Invent rhythm in all blank measures.

1. Articulate the rhythm of each voice on neutral syllables (da, ba, la, etc.) while employing the arm-beat patterns.

2. On each voice, improvise a major melody, then a minor melody, using a variety of intervals and ending on tonic while using arm beats.

3. Improvise a minor melody on the soprano voice using a variety of intervals and ending on tonic while clapping the rhythm of the bass voice.

CLEF READING

On each exercise perform the tasks in the order given while conducting the meter. Use a metronome, beginning at a slow tempo and increasing the rate of speed daily. Invent your own articulation for exercises that are unedited.

1. Speak the rhythm on syllables that will produce the desired articulation.
2. Speak (not sing) the letter name of each note out loud in the designated clefs while observing the correct articulation.

MELODIES

1. Establish tonic and pulse before beginning. Sing each melody on a neutral syllable, scale degree numbers, or pitch names.
2. Use arm-beats while singing each melody.
3. Accompany selected melodies with an appropriate harmonization in various styles.
4. Before performing the alto clef melodies, read the pitch names in the proper rhythm, then sing.

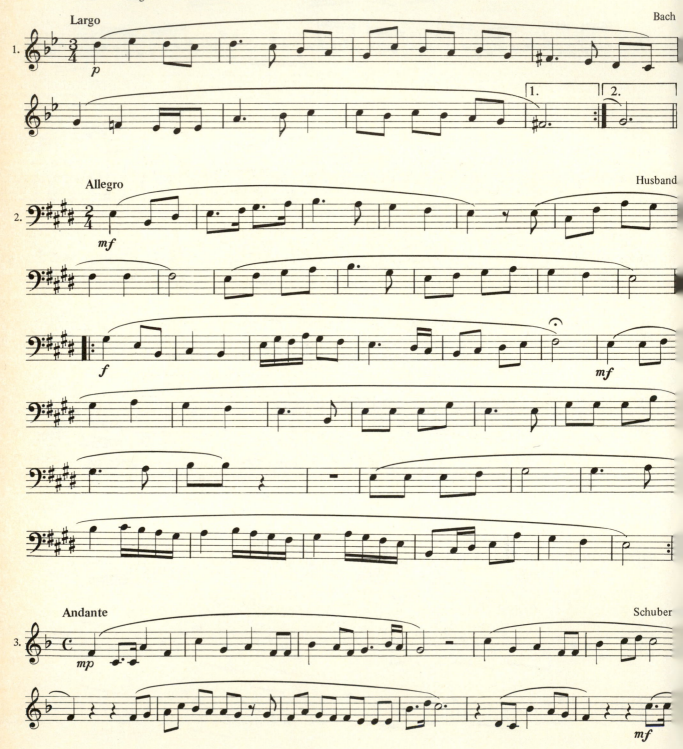

Allegro   *Anonymous*

21.

Canon   *Mozart*

22.

DUETS

1. Divide the class in half to perform duets.
2. Have two students perform duets.
3. Sing one line and clap the rhythm of the other.
4. Sing one line and perform the other on the piano (play and sing).

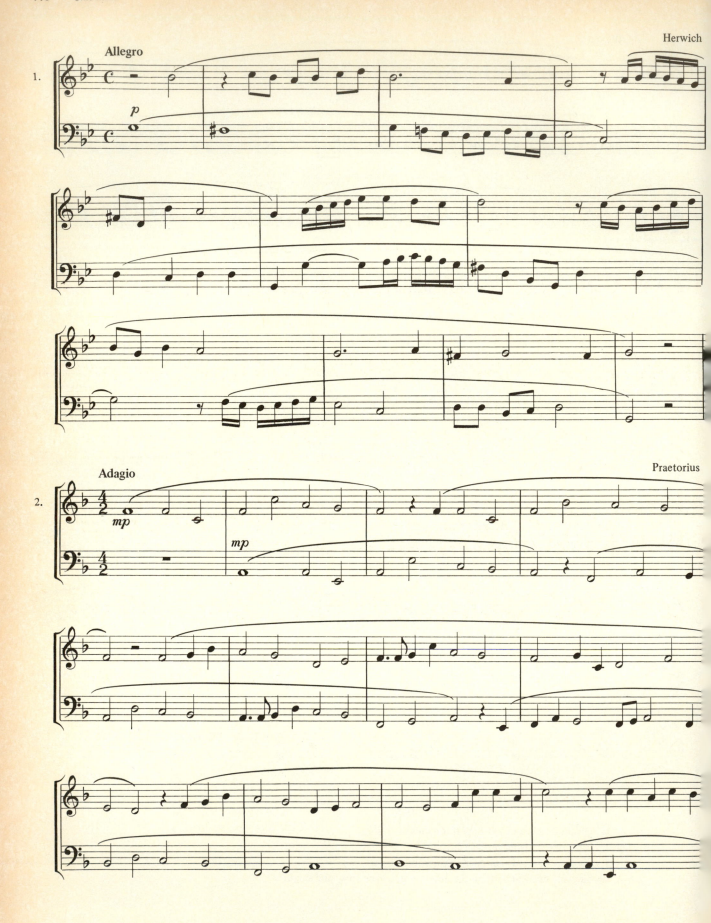

RHYTHM: *The Anacrusic Phrase*
PITCH: *Minor and Major Modes (Continued)*
CLEFS: *Treble, Bass, Alto, and Tenor*

RHYTHM: *The Anacrusic Phrase*

To this point, the phrase structure of each rhythm and melody has been crusic. That is, the phrase begins on the crusic partial of the crusic beat. This unit is an exploration into the infinite varieties of phrase lengths that are anacrusic; where the phrase may begin on any beat or any partial other than the crusic partial of the crusic beat.

Each anacrusic phrase is made up of three parts: the anacrusis, the crusis, and the metacrusis. The anacrusis is that portion of the phrase where the rhythm, melody and harmony all combine to give one the sensation of preparing for the crusis. The crusis is the point at which all of the musical elements combine to effect the dominant stress of the phrase. The crusis is not measurable in terms of time. Once the crusic moment has been effected, the metacrusis of the phrase is begun. The metacrusis, therefore, is a follow-through or fulfillment of the musical thought.

Upon examination of the rhythm reading exercises, one notices that a dotted phrase mark is used to indicate the phrase length and that the beaming of the note values relates to the phrase markings. Look carefully at the first complete measure of the first exercise (page 114). Notice that the last two eighth notes are separated by flags so that the first eighth marks the end of one phrase while the second eighth marks the beginning of the next phrase.

The phrase marks and beaming techniques also help the musician to perform the phrase with proper articulation and breath control. In the execution of the exercises, the phrasing must be observed and practiced.

PITCH: *Minor and Major Modes (Continued)*

PITCH EXERCISES

1. Sing each note as the root (1 3 5 3 1), third (3 1 3 5 3), or fifth (5 3 1 3 5) of major, minor, diminished, and augmented triads.

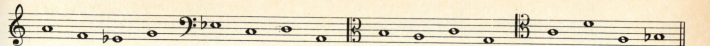

2. Play and match each pitch. Then sing the designated interval above or below the given note. Use a neutral syllable and pitch names.

3. Establish each tonality and then sing the patterns on scale degree numbers.
   a. c natural minor: 5 3 2 1↑ 6 5 8 7 6 5 3 4↓ 7 1 4 3 2 1
   b. b melodic minor: 5 6 7 8↓6 5 3 4 5 6↓7 1 2 3 4 5 6 5↓7 1 2 3 2 1
   c. d harmonic minor: 1 3 5 5 6 5↑7 8↓6 5 6 7 8 5 3 4↓7 1↑5 4 2 1

Perform the above patterns using the following anacrusic rhythmic patterns:

PITCH PATTERNS

Play the tonic pitch and establish the tonality by singing 1 3 5 3 1. Then sing the patterns on a neutral syllable, scale degree numbers, pitch names or solfeggio syllables.

Determine the tonality before proceeding as above.

RHYTHM READING I

On each exercise perform the tasks in the order given while employing the arm-beat pattern. Use a variety of tempi and dynamics.

1. Articulate the rhythm on neutral syllables.
2. Improvise a major melody and then a minor melody using a variety of intervals and ending on tonic. Use a variety of tonalities.

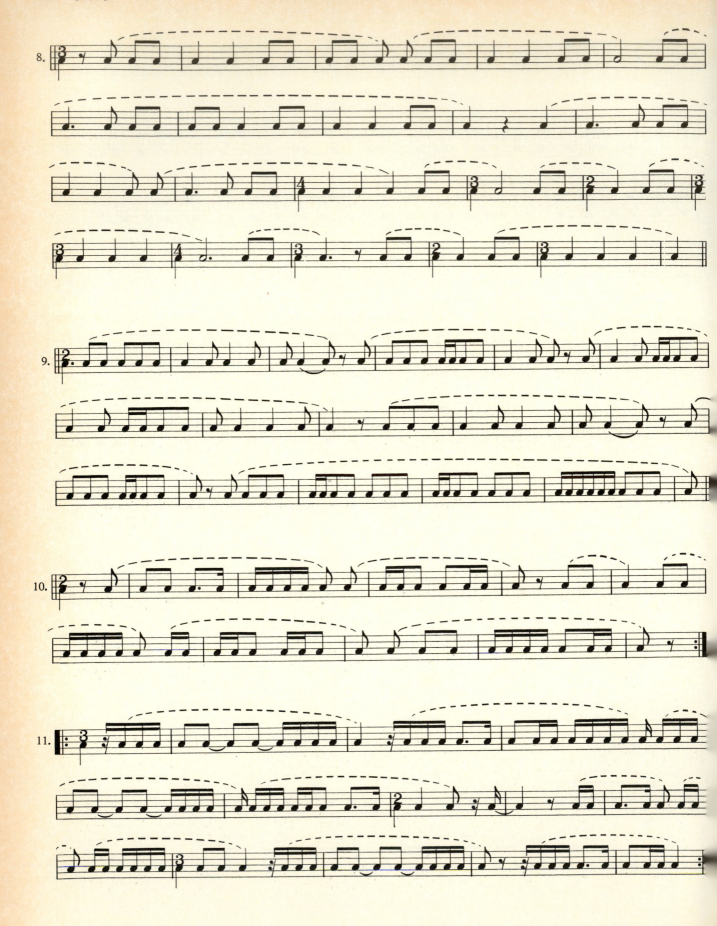

RHYTHM READING II

On each exercise perform the tasks in the order given. Use a variety of tempi and dynamics. Invent rhythm in all blank measures.

1. Articulate the rhythm of each voice on neutral syllables while employing the arm-beat pattern.

2. On each voice, improvise a major and then a minor melody using a variety of intervals and ending on tonic while employing the arm-beat pattern.

3. Improvise a minor melody on the soprano line using a variety of intervals and ending on tonic while clapping the rhythm of the bass.

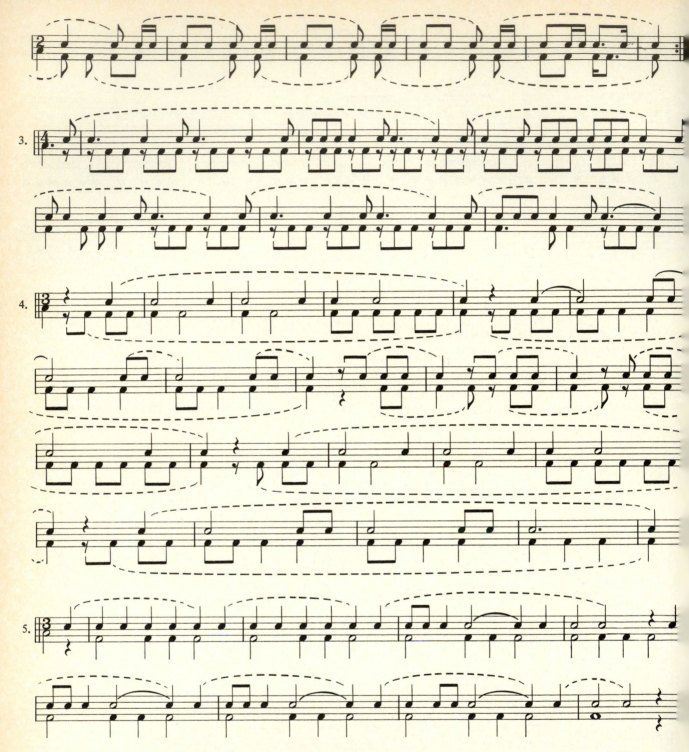

CLEF READING

On each exercise, perform the tasks in the order given while using the arm-beat pattern. Use a metronome, beginning at a slow tempo and increasing the rate of speed daily. Invent your own articulation for exercises that are unedited.

1. Speak the rhythm on syllables that best produce the desired articulation.
2. Speak (not sing) the letter name of each note out loud in the designated clefs while observing the correct articulation.

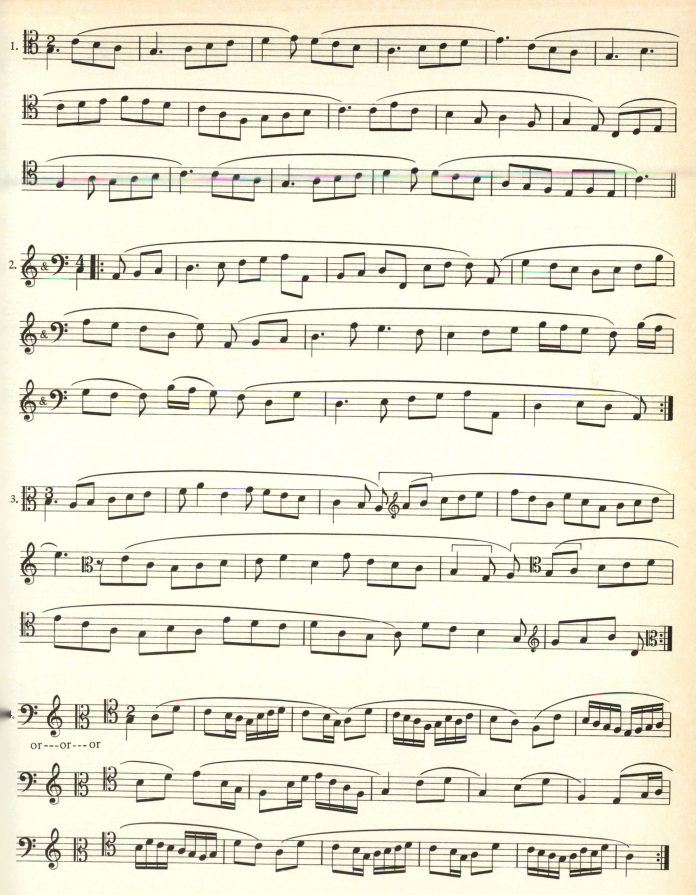

or---or---or

MELODIES

1. Establish tonic and pulse before beginning. Sing each melody on a neutral syllable, scale degree numbers, pitch names, or solfeggio syllables.
2. Conduct each melody while singing.
3. Accompany selected melodies with an appropriate harmonization in various styles.
4. Before performing the alto and tenor clef melodies, read the pitch names in the proper rhythm, then sing.

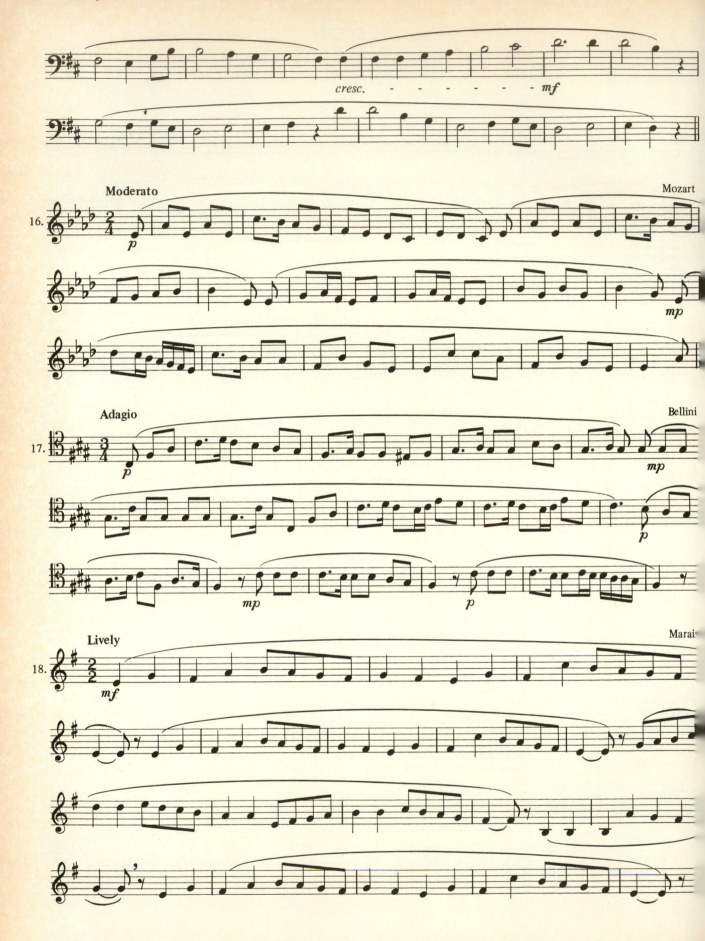

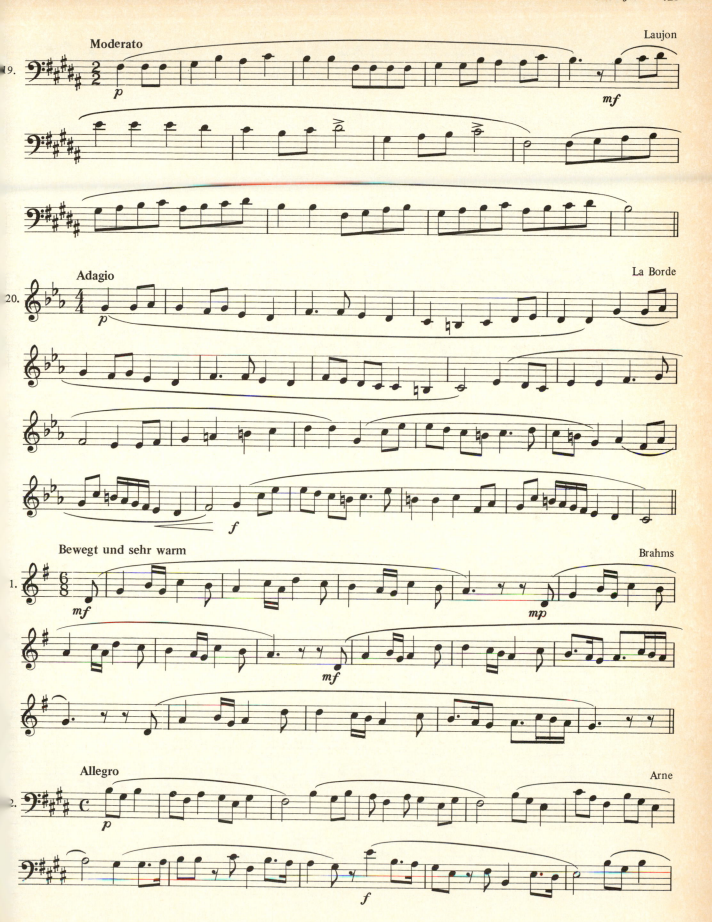

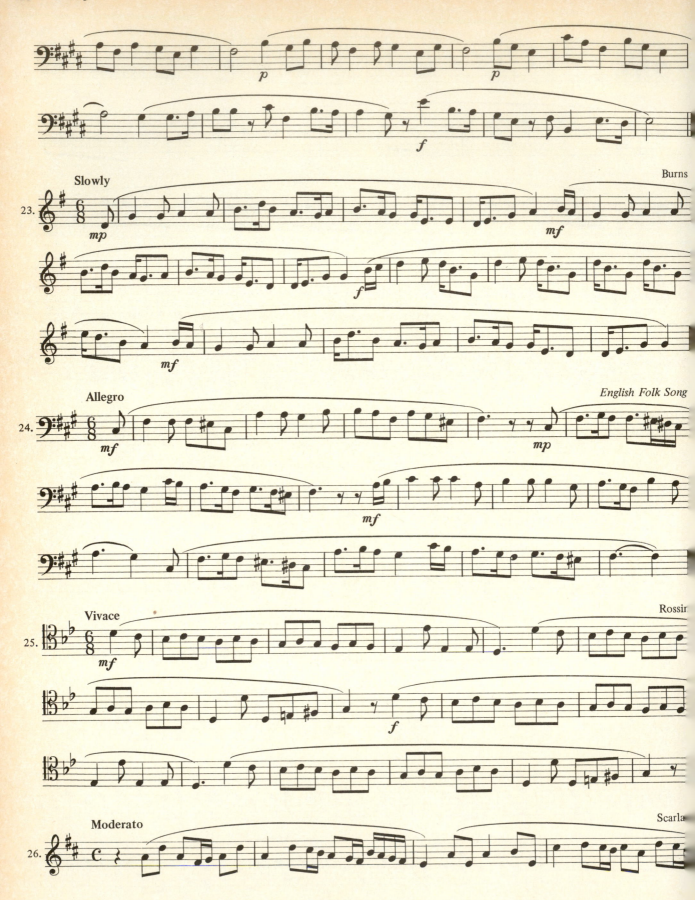

French Folk Song

30. Allegro   *mf*   *mp*   *mf*   *mp*

DUETS

1. Divide the class in half to perform the duets.
2. Have two students perform the duets.
3. Sing one line and clap the rhythm of the other.
4. Sing one line and perform the other on the piano (play and sing).

Cesti

1. Andante   *p*   *p*   *mf*   *mf*

RHYTHM: *Changing Meter (Simple/Compound)*
PITCH: *Review of Major and Minor Mode*
CLEFS: *Treble, Bass, Alto, Tenor, and Changing Clef*

RHYTHM: *Changing Meter (Simple/Compound)*

Changing meter is the result of an inconsistency in the distance from one crusic stress to another within a composition. This unit will deal with rhythmic phrases where the beat-note value of the meter changes back and forth from simple division [♩ ♪] to compound division [♩. ♪]. Therefore, the relationship from measure to measure can be established in one of two ways: beat to beat, [♩ = ♩.]; or division to division, [♪ = ♪] or [♪ = ♪] or [♩ = ♩].

In example 1, the metric indicators [♩. = ♩] instruct the performer to maintain a beat [♩]-to-beat [♩.] relationship in both meter changes. Since the tempo of the [♩.] is to be the tempo of the [♩], the music will sound giving no indication of any change of beat-note value.

ex. 1

However, in example 2, where the division of the beats are sounding, the change of the beat-note value is audibly evident. The tempo of the beat is constant but the tempo of the divisions is not.

ex. 2

In example 3, the metric indicators instruct the performer to maintain the tempo of the *divisions* throughout the composition. This type of metric relationship is most common in the folk music of Eastern Europe. With each metric change the distance between beats changes while the division remains constant.

ex. 3

PITCH: *Major and Minor Modes*

1. Sing major, natural minor, harmonic minor, and melodic minor scales ascending and descending in various tonalities using the following rhythmic patterns. Use scale degree numbers and arm-beat patterns. Repeat the rhythmic pattern until tonic is reached on the last note of the pattern.

2. Play the given pitch. Then sing the interval progression. You should end up on the last pitch. Use a neutral syllable.

   a. first pitch: E ↑M3 ↓M2 ↓P4 ↑m7 ↓m3 last pitch: G♯
   b. first pitch: F ↑P5 ↓m2 ↑m3 ↓P5 ↑P4 last pitch: C
   c. first pitch: B♭ ↑m7 ↓m2 ↓m2 ↓P4 ↑m3 last pitch: E
   d. first pitch: F♯ ↓m3 ↑°5 ↓m2 ↑P4 ↓M2 last pitch: B
   e. first pitch: E♭ ↑P4 ↑P4 ↓m2 ↓m7 ↑m2 last pitch: E♭

3. Sing the following patterns on scale degree numbers and on neutral syllables. Establish each tonality by singing the tonic triad.

   a. d melodic minor: 1 3 5 ↑ 7 8 ↓ 3 4 2 5 ↓ 7 1
   b. G major: 8 7 6 5 8 ↓ 4 5 3 4 5 ↓ 1 3 6 ↓ 7 1
   c. e natural minor: 1 7 1 3 5 6 5 8 4 6 5 3 2 7 1 8
   d. D♭ major: 3 5 1 ↑ 6 5 ↑ 2 1 ↓ 5 6 3 4 2 1
   e. c harmonic minor: 8 7 8 ↓ 6 5 4 5 3 4 ↓ 7 1 ↑ 6 5 6 7 8

4. Perform the following two-part exercises as suggested below:

   a. perform the top line on neutral syllables or scale degree numbers.
   b. clap the accompanying complementary rhythm.
   c. sing the melodic material in major and various minor tonalities.

Moderato

Slowly

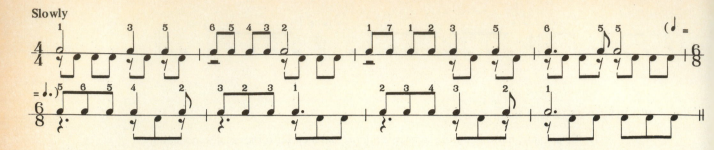

PITCH PATTERNS

Play the tonic pitch and establish tonic by singing 1 3 5 3 1. Then sing the pitch patterns on a neutral syllable, scale degree numbers, pitch names, or solfeggio syllables.

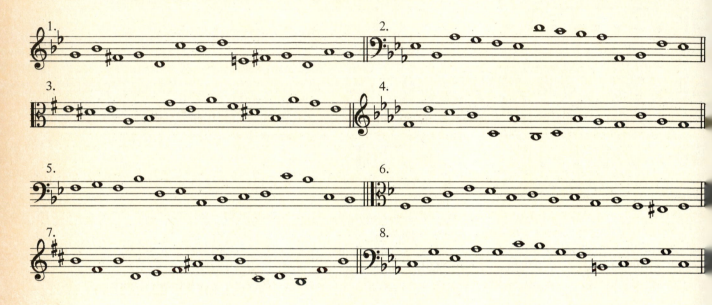

Determine the tonality before proceeding as above.

RHYTHM READING I

On each exercise perform the tasks in the order given. Use a variety of tempi. Invent rhythm in all blank measures and use dynamics.

1. Articulate the rhythm on neutral syllables (da, ba, la, etc.) while

> clapping the divisions.
>
> clapping the beat.
>
> employing the arm-beat pattern.

2. While using the arm-beat pattern, improvise a major melody, then a minor melody, using a variety of intervals and ending on tonic. Use a variety of tonalities.

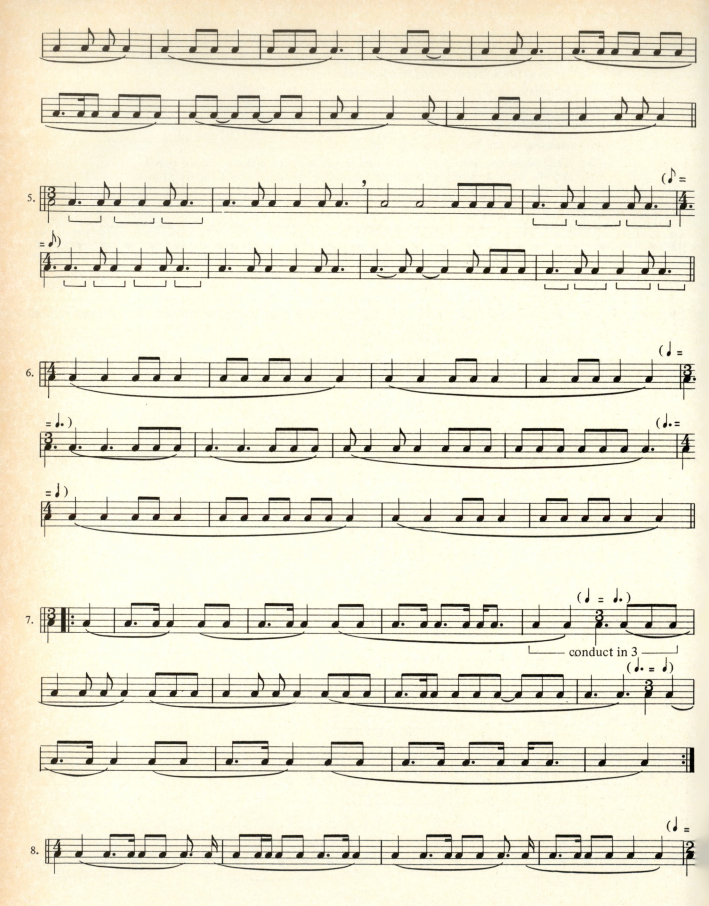

conduct in 3

RHYTHM READING II

On each exercise perform the tasks in the order given. Use a variety of tempi and dynamics.

1. Articulate the rhythm of each voice on neutral syllables while

   clapping the divisions.
   clapping the beat.
   employing the arm-beat pattern.

2. On each voice, improvise a major melody, then a minor melody, using a variety of intervals and ending on tonic while conducting the meter.

3. Improvise a minor melody on the soprano voice using a variety of intervals and ending on tonic. Clap the rhythm of the bass voice.

CLEF READING

On each exercise perform the tasks in the order given. Use a metronome, beginning at a slow tempo and increasing the rate of speed daily. Invent your own articulation for exercises that are unedited.

1. Speak the rhythm on syllables that best produce the desired articulation while

    clapping the division.

    clapping the beat.

    employing the arm-beat pattern.

2. Speak (not sing) the letter name of each note out loud in the designated clefs while observing the correct articulation and using the proper arm-beat pattern.

MELODIES

1. Establish tonic and pulse before beginning. Sing each melody on neutral syllables, scale degree numbers, pitch names, or solfeggio syllables.

2. Employ arm-beat gestures while singing each melody.

3. Accompany each melody with an appropriate harmonization in various styles.

Note: The equivalencies indicated at the beginning of a melody will remain in effect throughout the melody unless otherwise stated.

4. Before performing the alto and tenor clef melodies, read the pitch names in proper rhythm, then sing.

Old German Tune

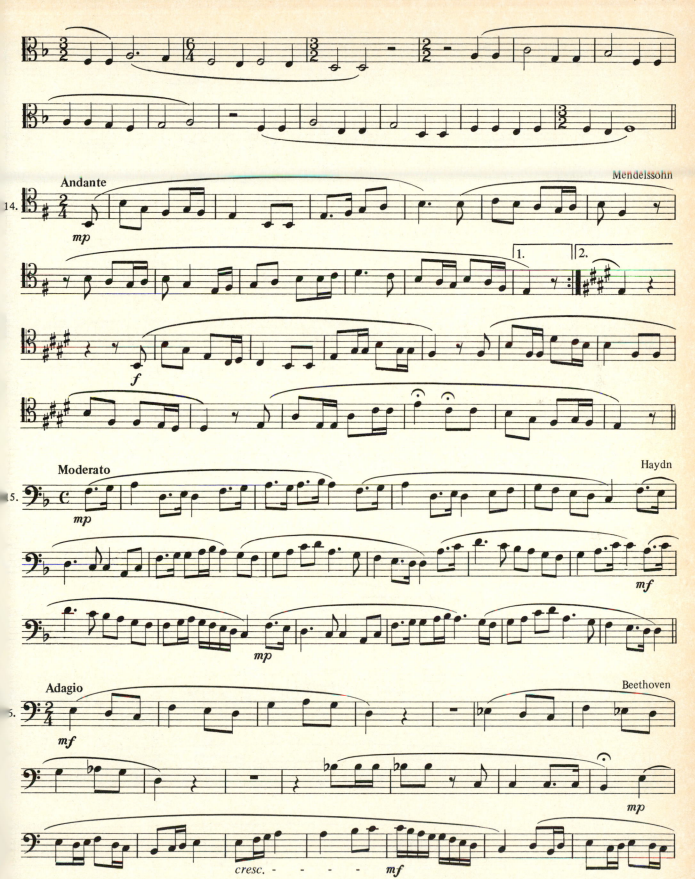

DUETS

1. Divide the class in half to perform duets.
2. Have two students perform duets.
3. Sing one line and clap the rhythm of the other.
4. Sing one line and perform the other on the piano (play and sing).

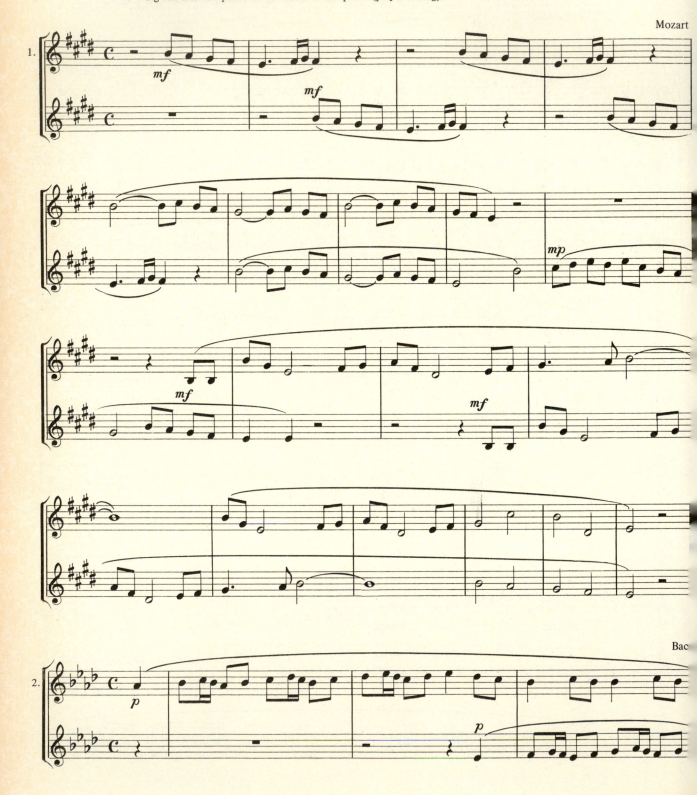

RHYTHM: *The Beat (Irregular Division—Part I)*
PITCH: *Chromatic Passing and Neighbor Tones*
CLEFS: *Treble, Bass, Alto, Tenor, and Changing Clef*

RHYTHM: *The Beat (Irregular Division—Part I)*

It has already been well established that beats are normally divided either by two in simple meter (simple division) or by three in compound meter (compound division). *Irregular division* is a term applied to selected beats which are divided into more or fewer partials than that designated by the meter signature.

This unit will deal only with two types of irregular divisions: The *triplet*, [♪♪♪³], [³♪♪♪], [♩ ♩ ♩³], and the *duplet*, [♪♪²], [♪♪²], [♩ ♩²]. The triplet exists only in simple meter when there are three divisions in a beat instead of the usual two. The duplet exists only in compound meter when there are two divisions in a beat instead of the usual three. Study the following chart.

SIMPLE DIVISION			COMPOUND DIVISION		
beat note	simple division	irregular division	beat note	compound division	irregular division
♪	♬	♬³	♪.	♬♬	♬²
♩	♫	♩♩♩³	♩.	♩♩♩	♩♩²
𝅗𝅥	♩ ♩	♩ ♩ ♩³	𝅗𝅥.	♩ ♩ ♩	♩ ♩²

PITCH: *Chromatic Passing and Neighbor Tones*

Units 1 through 9 have dealt exclusively with diatonic material; that is, material which is confined to notes which are in the given key. The only chromaticism has been in material that has the harmonic or melodic scale as its basis.

Unit 10 will gradually introduce, stepwise, chromatic material in the form of chromatic passing tones and neighbor tones. The chromatics used here do not imply a change of chord (as do the secondary dominant chromatics in the next unit), but rather occur within the same harmonic framework or between two different implied harmonies.

PITCH EXERCISES
Chromatic Passing and Neighbor Tones

1. *Using pitch names,* match each given pitch. Then:

   a. Add a chromatic neighbor tone above and return to the given pitch.

   b. Add a chromatic neighbor tone below and return to the given pitch.

   c. Add a chromatic passing tone above and continue up one half step.

   d. Add a chromatic passing tone below and continue down one half step.

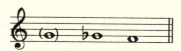

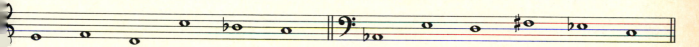

2. Sing each pattern on scale degree numbers. Then perform the exercise again, repeating each pitch and adding either chromatic upper neighbors or lower neighbors between each repeated note.

   a. C major: 1 3 5 6 4 5 7 1
   b. D major: 5 3 4 2 1 6 5 3 1
   c. b♭ minor: 1 5 4 2 1 8 5 3 2 1
   d. f minor: 3 4 5 ♮7 1 3 2 5 1

3. Sing each pattern on scale degree numbers. Then perform the exercise again, adding chromatic passing tones between the numbers that are bracketed.

   a. A major: 1̄ 2̄ 3 5 6̄ 5 3 4̄ 5 6 4̄ 2̄ 1
   b. e minor: 5 6̄ 5 4 3 2 1 5 6 2 3̄ 4̄ 5 ↓ ♯7 1
   c. B♭ major: 3 4̄ 5 3 4 2̄ 1 6̄ 5 7 8 6̄ 5 3 2 1
   d. a minor: 1 3 5̄ 4 3 1 2̄ 4 6 5 4̄ 2̄ 1

4. Establish the tonality by singing 1 3 5 3 1. Then, perform the following patterns on scale degree numbers and/or neutral syllables

   a. E♭ major: 1 3 5 ♯4 5 3 6 5 8 ↓ 3 ♭3 2 1 7 1
   b. A major: 8 5 ♭5 4 3 2 1 5 ♭6 5 ♯5 6 7 5 8
   c. B♭ major: 5 3 4 2 ♭2 1 6 5 ♮4 5 3 ♮2 3 2 1
   d. e minor: 1 3 5 3 1 ♮2 1 6 5 ♯4 5 ♮4 ♭4 3 2 1

   Perform the above exercises on neutral syllables using the following rhythm patterns:

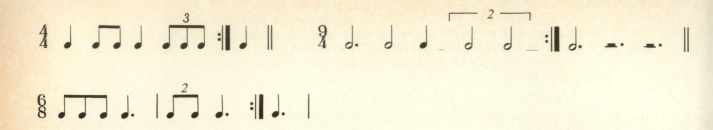

5. Perform the following melodies, improvising material in the blank measures. The improvised measures should remain rhythmically consistent with the rest of the melody. Try to use chromatic passing and neighbor tones in your improvised material.

PITCH PATTERNS

Establish each tonality by singing the tonic triad on 1 3 5 3 1. Then, perform each pitch pattern by singing it on numbers, letter names, neutral syllables, or solfeggio syllables. If using scale degree numbers, sing the chromatic pitches either on neutral syllables or as "sharp 4," "flat 3," etc.

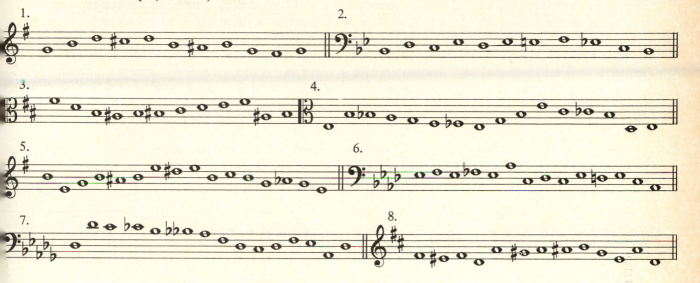

RHYTHM READING I

On each exercise perform the tasks in the order given. Use a variety of tempi and dynamics.

1. Articulate the rhythm on neutral syllables while

    clapping the beat.

    clapping the divisions.

    employing the arm-beat pattern.

2. While employing the arm-beat pattern,

    improvise on each exercise by arbitrarily replacing the note values for rests.

    improvise a major melody, then a minor melody, using a variety of intervals and ending on tonic. Use a variety of tonalities.

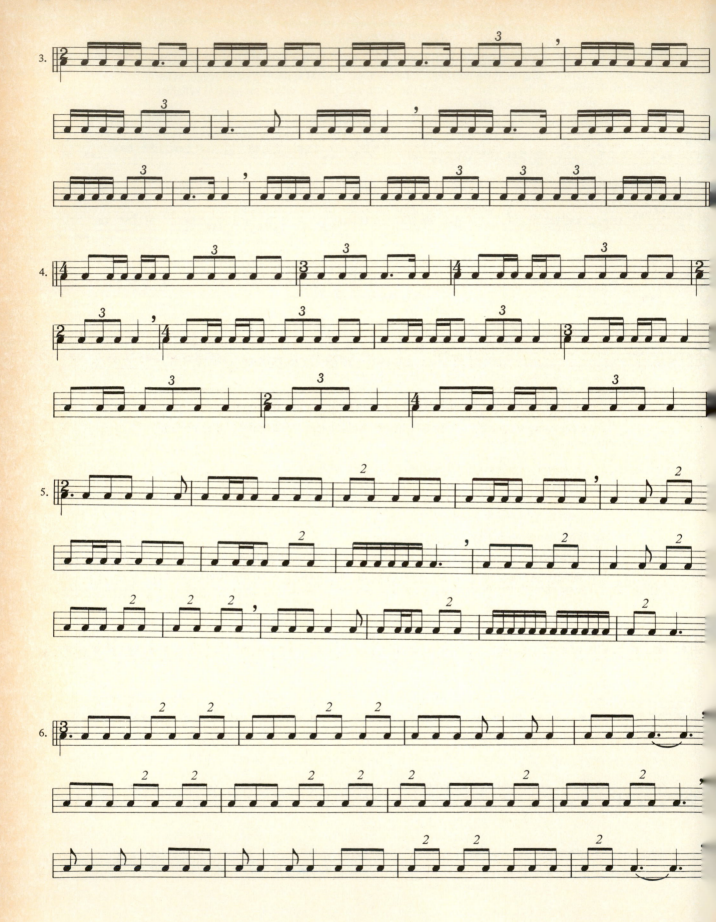

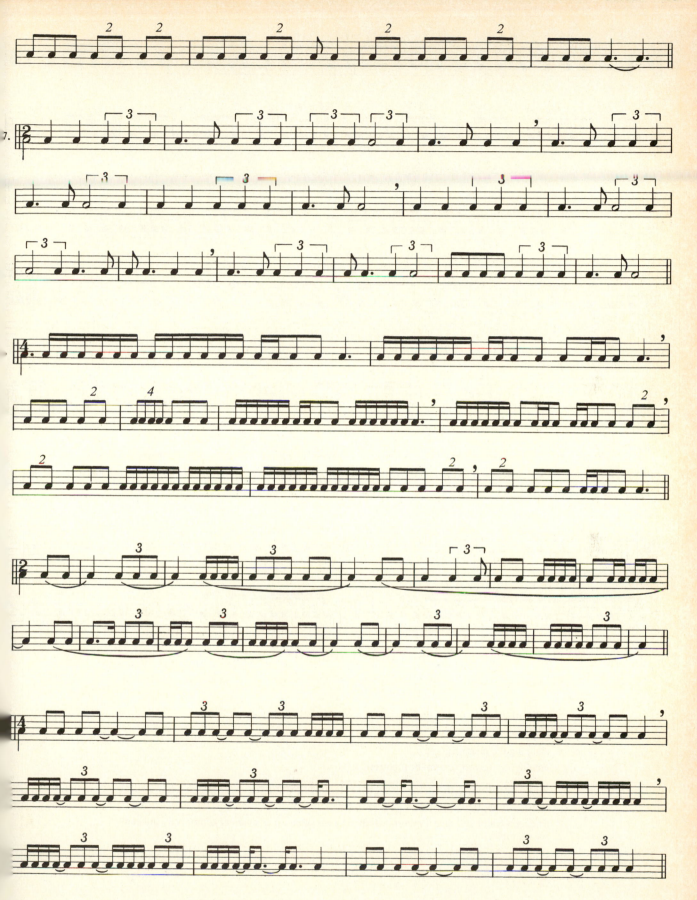

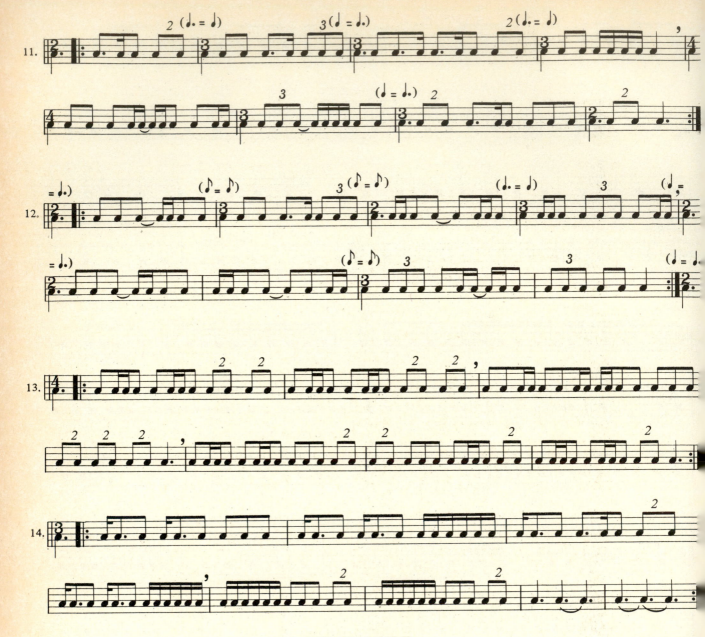

RHYTHM READING II

On each exercise perform the tasks in the order given. Use a variety of tempi and dynamics.

1. Articulate the rhythm of each voice on neutral syllables while

   clapping the beat.

   clapping the divisions.

   employing the proper arm-beat pattern.

2. While employing the arm-beat patterns, improvise by

   arbitrarily replacing the note values for rests.

   singing a major and then a minor melody on each voice using a variety of intervals and ending on tonic.

3. Sing a minor melody on the soprano voice using a variety of intervals and ending on tonic while clapping the rhythm of the bass voice.

4. Sing a major melody on the soprano voice using a variety of intervals and ending on tonic while clapping the rhythm of the bass voice.

CLEF READING

On each exercise perform the tasks in the order given. Use a metronome, beginning at a slow tempo and increasing the rate of speed daily. Invent your own articulation for exercises that are unedited.

1. Speak the rhythm on syllables that will best produce the desired articulation while

   clapping the beat.
   clapping the division.

   employing the arm-beat pattern.

2. Speak (not sing) the letter name of each note out loud in the designated clefs while observing the correct articulation and using the proper arm–beat pattern.

MELODIES

1. Establish tonic and pulse before beginning. Sing each melody on a neutral syllable, scale degree numbers, pitch names, or solfeggio syllables.
2. Use an appropriate arm-beat pattern.
3. Accompany selected melodies with an appropriate harmonization in various styles.

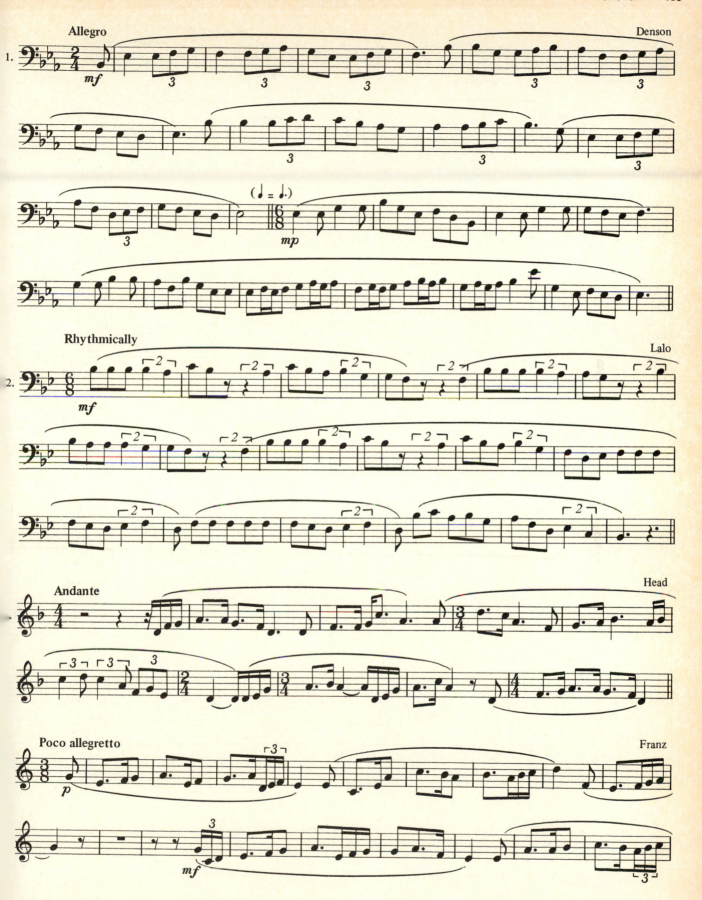

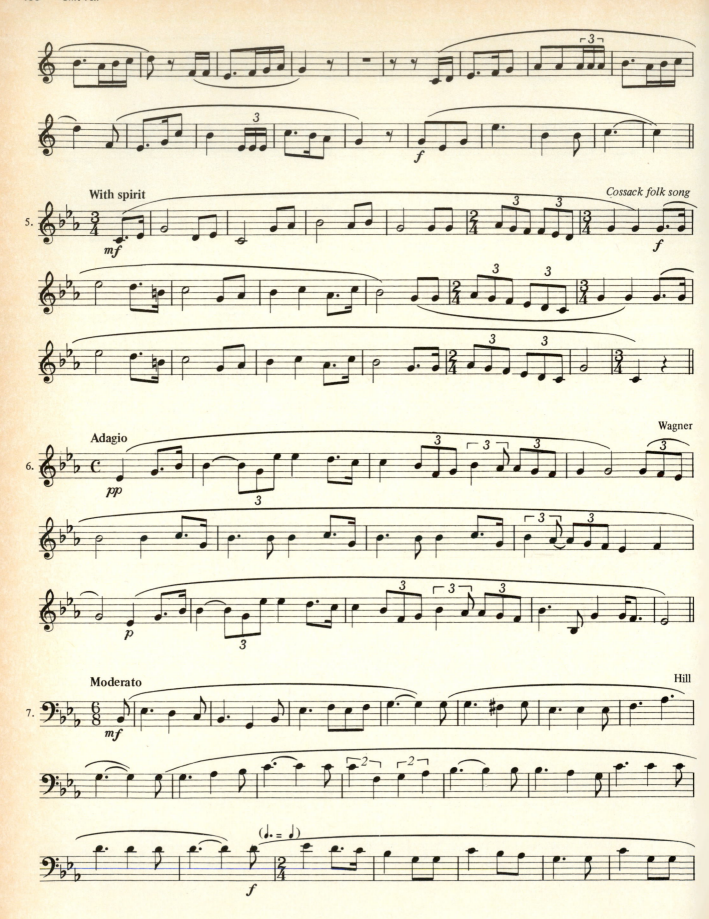

12. Moderato — Baumgartner

13. Andante — Mozart

14. Lively — Costa Rica

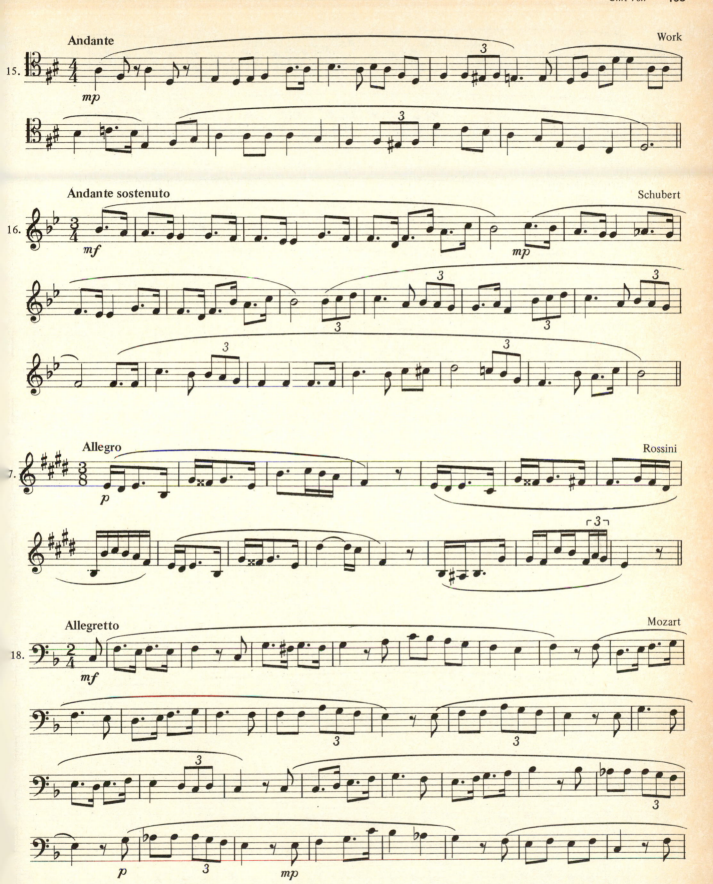

22. Andantino — Verdi

23. Allegro moderato — Rossini

DUETS

1. Divide the class in half to perform duets.
2. Have two students perform duets.
3. Sing one line and clap the rhythm of the other.
4. Sing one line and perform the other on the piano (play and sing).

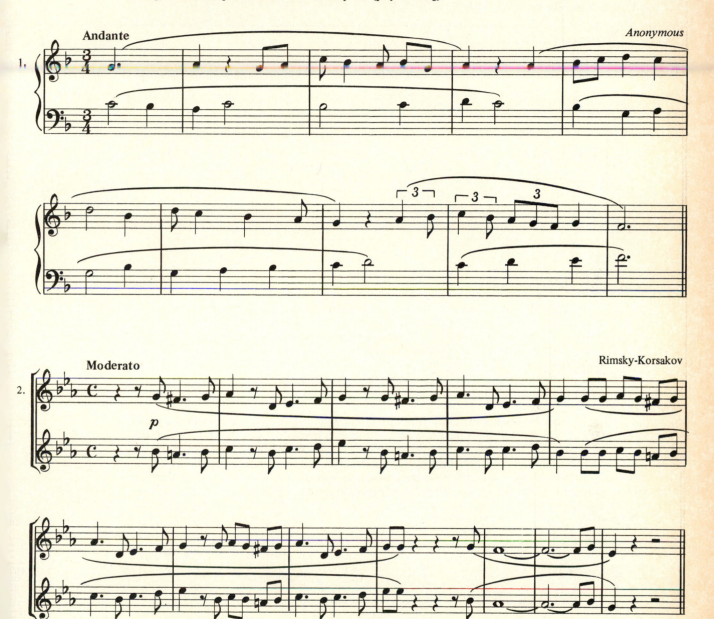

RHYTHM: *Syncopation (Inter-measure)*
PITCH: *Secondary Dominants*
CLEFS: *Treble, Bass, Tenor, Alto, and Changing Clef*

RHYTHM: *Syncopation (Inter-measure)*

Syncopation, as defined in unit 6, is the result of a rupture between meter and beat. Unit 6 also discussed retarded and anticipated syncopation. In this unit, *inter-measure syncopation* is introduced and can be defined as that type of syncopation that occurs over the barline. Inter-measure syncopation permits the first beat of the measure to be in either retarded syncopation or in anticipated syncopation. However, it is impossible to determine whether the inter-measure syncopation is anticipated or retarded without harmonic function and melodic line. The following illustrations are offered for analysis.

The following illustration is a perfect example of retarded inter-measure syncopation. The dotted lines illustrate how the music would sound if the treble voice were not displaced into syncopation behind the bass line. At the piano, one should play the two voices together as indicated by the dotted lines and then play the phrase as written. It is immediately apparent that the treble and bass are harmonically and melodically compatible. The composer, W. F. Bach, simply shifted the melodic line so that it would sound one half beat later than the bass.

(sounds late)   (resolution)

The next illustration demonstrates the use of inter-measure anticipated syncopation. The composer, Robert Schumann, displaced the melody so that it sounds one half beat earlier than the bass line. Again, the dotted lines aid the eye in placing the melody directly above the bass. One should perform the phrase both ways; first non-syncopated and then syncopated.

(sounds early)   (resolution)

PITCH: *Secondary Dominants*

The melodic material in unit 11 will focus on the use of the secondary dominant (or secondary embellishing chord). In harmonic terms, the secondary dominant seventh chord is a major-minor seventh chord, which resolves regularly up a perfect fourth. A chart helpful in remembering the scale degrees on which the various secondary dominants are built follows:

Secondary Dominant	built on the	resolves to scale degree number
V^7/IV (iv)*	first scale degree	4
V^7/V	second scale degree	5
V^7vi (VI)	third scale degree	6
V^7/ii	sixth scale degree	2
V^7/iii (III)	seventh scale degree	3

*in minor

Melodically, the secondary dominant generally manifests itself in one of two ways:

1. There is a raised pitch which acts as a new leading tone to an appropriate scale degree. This chromatic pitch will resolve up by half step to that scale degree.
2. There is a lowered pitch (the seventh of the secondary dominant seventh chord) which will resolve down by step.

It is important to remember that secondary dominants are momentary changes of key center. A chromatic pitch that occurs one time cannot really constitute a modulation. The secondary dominants in this unit, therefore, will involve the occurrence of a chromatic pitch which implies a chord change on the chromatic pitch itself (unlike the chromatic passing tones or neighbor tones in the previous unit which occurred within a single harmony or between two different harmonies). After the resolution of the altered pitch, there is an immediate return to the feeling of the original tonality or, in some cases, a moving on in sequence to another secondary dominant.

PITCH EXERCISES

1. Using the given note as the root (1), sing major-minor seventh chords. Use numbers and/or pitch names. After each, sing an appropriate resolution up a perfect fourth to a major or minor chord (see example).

example: given   sing 1 3 5 7 5 3 1   resolve 5 1 1 3 1   or 5 1 1 3 1

2. Establish the tonality using 1 3 5 3 1 and perform each pattern on scale degree numbers. Then sing the pattern again, adding a secondary dominant seventh chord at each asterisk that will embellish the following note. The root of the secondary dominant will always be the same as the number before each asterisk (consult the chart on page 169).

    a. D major: 1 2 3 2 * 5 3 * 6 5 1
    b. c minor: 1 * 4 3 2 1(♭)7 * 3 4 5 1
    c. E♭ major: 1 3 5 1 ↓ 6 * 2 ↑ 5 1 7 * 3 4 5 1
    d. a minor: 1 3 5 3 * 6 5 1 * 4 5 6 5 ↓ ♯7 1

3. Establish the tonality using 1 3 5 3 1 and perform each pattern on scale degree numbers. Then sing each pattern again, adding a leading tone before each asterisked pitch. This will imply a secondary dominant of that note. Perform each added leading tone on a neutral syllable or as "♯4," "♯3," etc.

    a. E major: 1 3 5 *2 3 *6 4 5 1
    b. a minor: 8 5 6 *5 3 1 *4 6 5 *2 1
    c. B♭ minor: 3 4 5 *3 6 *5 *2 *6 4 5 ↓ 7 1
    d. g minor: 1 ↓ 5 1 ↑ *5 3 4 2 ♯7 1

4. Establish the tonality using 1 3 5 3 1. Then perform the following patterns on a neutral syllable, scale degree numbers, or pitch names.

    a. D major: 1 3 5 3 ♯4 5 ♯1 2 3 5 1
    b. B♭ major: 8 7 8 5 8 ♭7 6 5 3 ♮4 5 3 4 2 1
    c. a minor: 3 4 5 1 ♯3 4 2 5 1 8 ♯4 5 3 2 1
    d. d minor: 1 3 5 ♯4 5 ♯7 8 ♮7 6 5 3 4 5 ♯7 1

5. Perform the following melodies, improvising material in the blank measures. The improvised material should remain consistent, melodically and rhythmically, with the rest of the melody. Try to use chromatics that imply secondary dominants in your improvisation.

a.

b.

PITCH PATTERNS

Study each pitch pattern to determine the location of any secondary dominants or clef changes. Then establish the tonality of each and sing on a neutral syllable, scale degree numbers, pitch names, or solfeggio syllables.

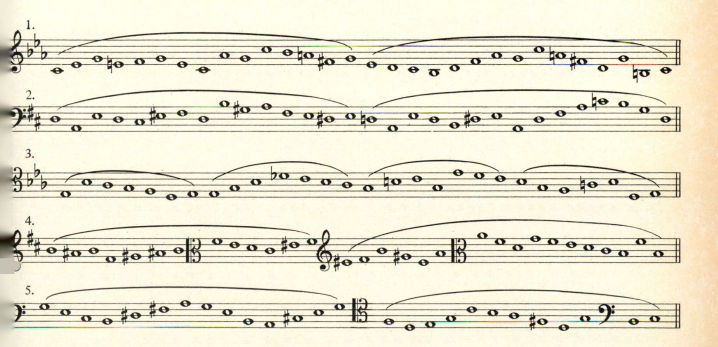

RHYTHM READING I

On each exercise perform the tasks in the order given while employing the arm-beat pattern. Use a variety of tempi and dynamics.

1. Articulate the rhythm on neutral syllables.
2. Improvise a major melody and then a minor melody using a variety of intervals and ending on tonic. Use a variety of tonalities.

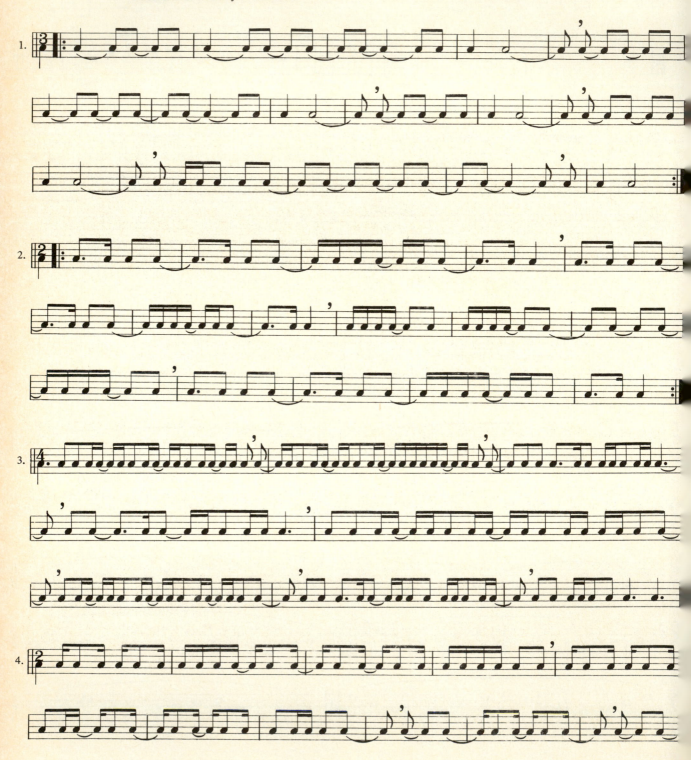

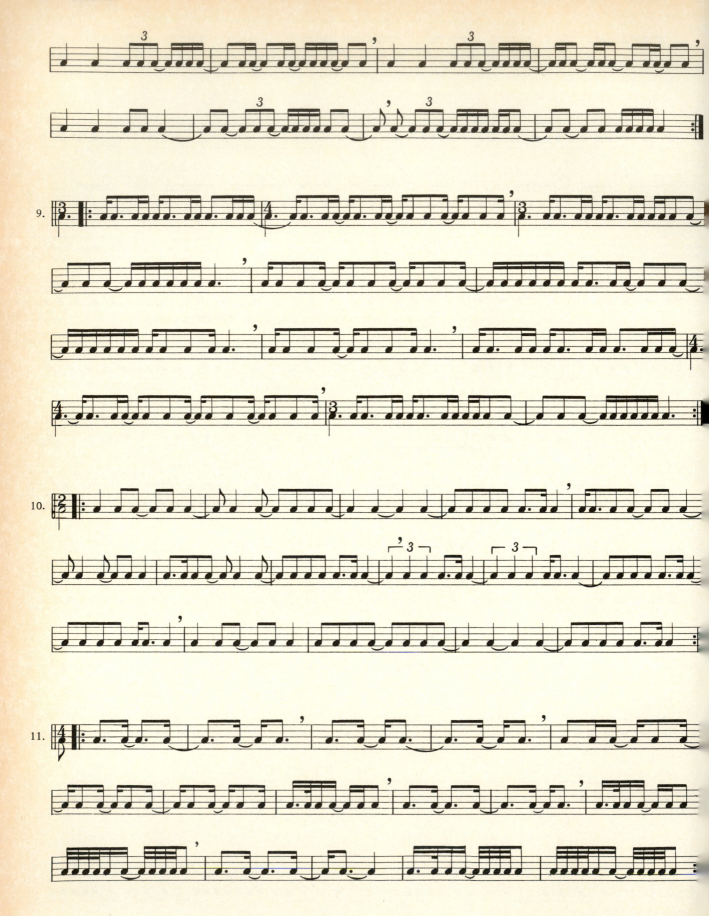

12.

RHYTHM READING II

On each exercise perform the tasks in the order given. Use a variety of tempi and dynamics.

1. Articulate the rhythm of each voice on neutral syllables while employing the arm–beat pattern.

2. On each voice, improvise a major and then a minor melody using a variety of intervals and ending on tonic. Employ the arm-beat pattern.

3. Improvise a major and then a minor melody on the soprano line using a variety of intervals ending on tonic. Clap the rhythm of the bass.

CLEF READING

On each exercise, perform the tasks in the order given while using the arm-beat pattern. Use a metronome, beginning at a slow tempo and increasing the rate of speed daily. Invent your own articulation for exercise that are unedited.

1. Speak the rhythm on syllables that best produce the desired articulation.
2. Speak (not sing) the letter name of each note out loud in the designated clefs while observing the correct articulation.

MELODIES

1. Establish tonic and pulse before beginning. Sing each melody on a neutral syllable, scale degree numbers, pitch names, or solfeggio syllables (see melodies 1 and 4 for secondary dominant analysis).

2. Use arm–beat patterns while singing.
3. Accompany selected melodies with appropriate harmonizations (including secondary dominants) in various styles.

Rossini

9. Allegro

Telemann

10. Vivace

Canon ① ② Mozart

11.

Andante

15.

Andante moderato

16.

Un poco allegretto

17.

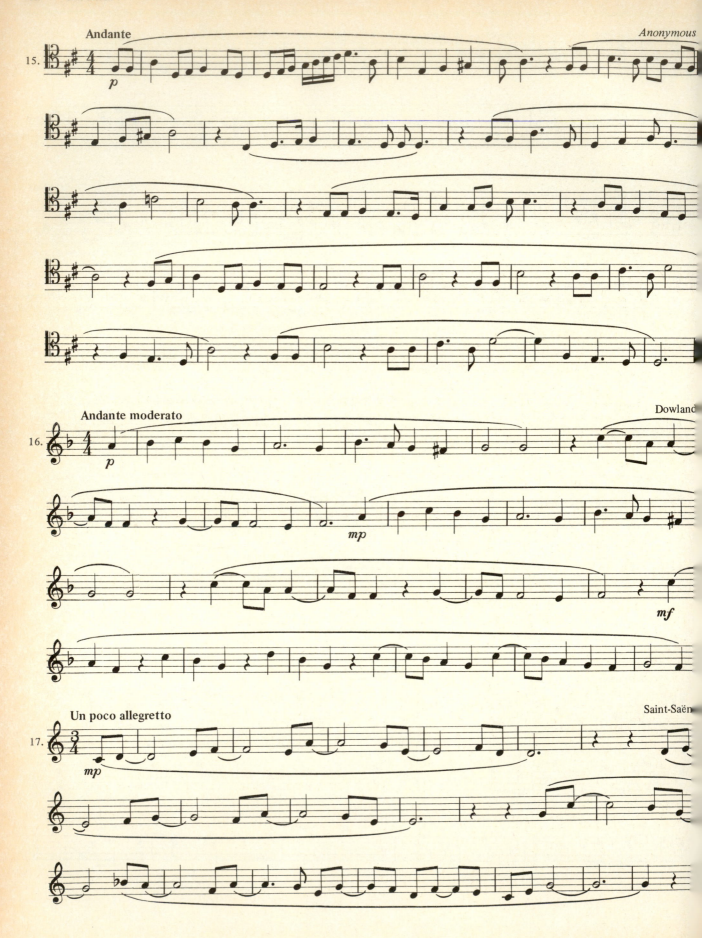

Allegretto moderato — Morley

Allegro ma non troppo — Corkine

Andantino — Halèvy

Poco allegro — Schubert

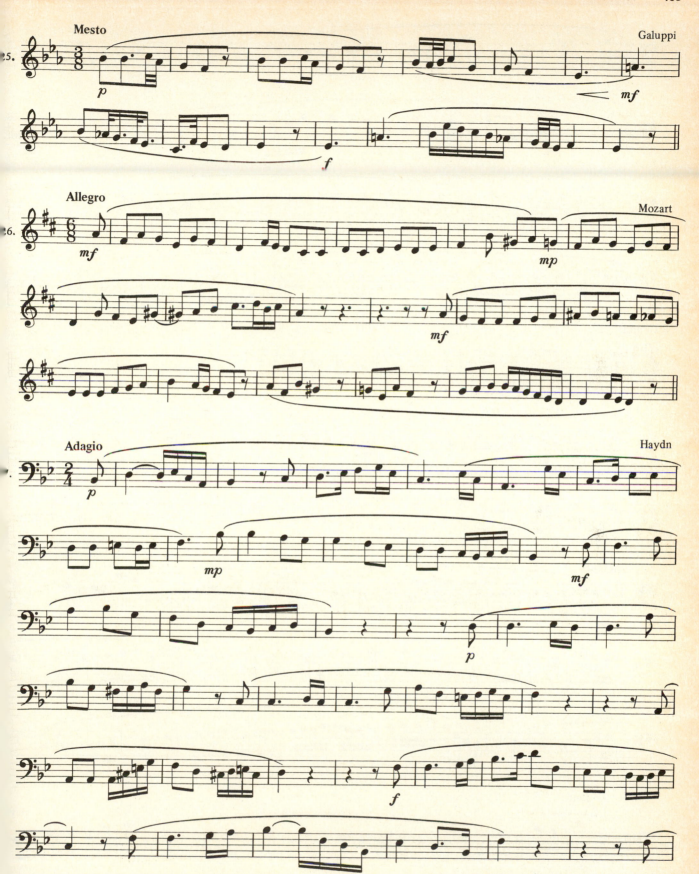

Canon   Haydn

28.

Andante   Haydn

29.

Andante   Haydn

30.

DUETS

1. Divide the class in half to perform duets.
2. Have two students perform the duets.
3. Sing one line and clap the rhythm of the other.
4. Sing one line and perform the other on the piano (play and sing).

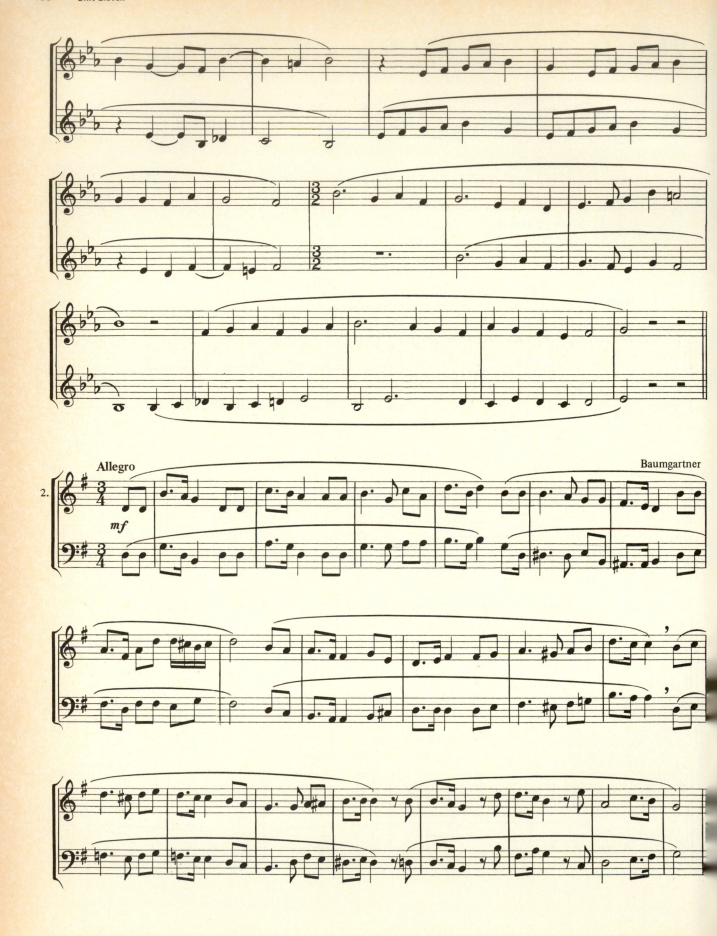

Allegro

2.

mf

Baumgartner

Andante

Blow

RHYTHM: *The Beat (Irregular Division—Part II)*
PITCH: *Modulation to the Dominant and Subdominant*
CLEFS: *Treble, Bass, Alto, Tenor, and Changing Clef*

RHYTHM: *The Beat*
(Irregular Division—Part II)

As previously discussed in unit 10, *irregular division* is a term applied to those beats that are occasionally divided into more or fewer partials than designated by the meter signature.

This unit continues the work introduced in unit 10 by dealing with the *quadruplet* [♩♩♩♩], the *quintuplet* [♩♩♩♩♩], the *sextuplet* [♩♩♩♩♩♩], and the *septuplet* [♩♩♩♩♩♩♩]. Study the following chart, which illustrates the relative values of regular and irregular divisions.

PITCH: *Modulation to the Dominant and Subdominant*

The melodic portion of units 12 through 15 will focus on modulations to both near-related and distantly related keys. Melodically, an effective modulation should consist of two processes:

1. chromatic change(s) which will imply a change of key signature to a different key (chromatic inflection) and

2. the establishment of the new key by means of a focus on the new tonic and its triad.

The most effective way of successfully performing most modulations to near-related keys is to find a pitch common to both keys. To choose the best note to use as a pivot, find the chromatic alteration and then the closest preceding note common to both keys. Then, mentally change your pitch orientation on that note toward the new tonic.

PITCH EXERCISES

1. Establish the initial key by singing 1 3 5 3 1. Then perform the following modulating exercises on scale degree numbers. When reaching the pivot tone, repeat that pitch using both scale degree numbers. Before beginning each exercise, determine which scale degree in the second key will be altered (in the first example, the chromatic alteration when modulating from C to G will be from f to f♯, which is 7 in the key of G).

   a. C major: 1 7 1 3 5 6 5 8↓|3
               G major: |6 7 8 6 5 6 7 8↓3 4 5 8

   b. B♭ major: 3 4 5 1↑6 5 8↓3|4
               E♭ major:|1 2 3 4 5.3 4 2 1↑6 5 3 4↓7 1

   c. g minor: 1 5 1 ♯7 1 ♮7 6 5↑1 3 5 3|2
               d minor:|5 4 3 2 1 ♯7 1↑5 6 5 8 5 3 2 1

   d. e minor: 1 3 5 2 3 2 1 5 8 7|6
               a minor:|3 2 1 ♯7 1↓5↑3 2 1 3 5↓♯7 1↓5 6 4 5 5↑1

2. Before beginning, study each melody to determine the initial and final tonalities and determine which chromatic pitch will imply a change to the second tonality. Then, establish the initial key and perform each melody, filling in the blank measures with modulating material. Keep the new material rhythmically consistent with the rest of the melody.

3. **Continue each of the following melodies in the style established, modulating to the specified key. Before beginning, determine the necessary chromatic change(s) and their relationship to both the initial and final tonal centers. Be sure to establish the second key.**

a)

G:

Improvise two more phrases modulating to D major.

b)

b:

Improvise two more phrases modulating to e minor.

c)

f:

Improvise two more phrases modulating to c minor.

PITCH PATTERNS

Study each pitch pattern to determine beginning and final tonality. Choose a possible pivot tone and determine its scale degree function in each key. Then perform the pattern on a neutral syllable, scale degree numbers, pitch names, or solfeggio syllables. If using scale degree numbers, repeat the pivot note using the scale degree number in both keys.

1.

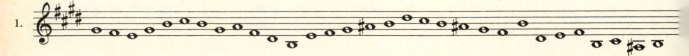

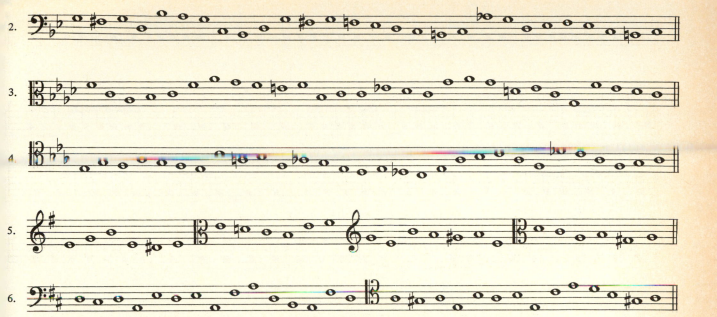

RHYTHM READING I

On each exercise perform the tasks in the order given. Use a variety of tempi and dynamics.

1. Articulate the rhythm on neutral syllables while

   clapping the beat.

   clapping the divisions.

   employing the arm-beat pattern.

2. While employing the arm-beat pattern,

   improvise on each exercise by arbitrarily replacing the note values for rests.

   improvise a major melody, then a minor melody, using a variety of intervals and ending on tonic. Replace beats with rests and use a variety of tonalities.

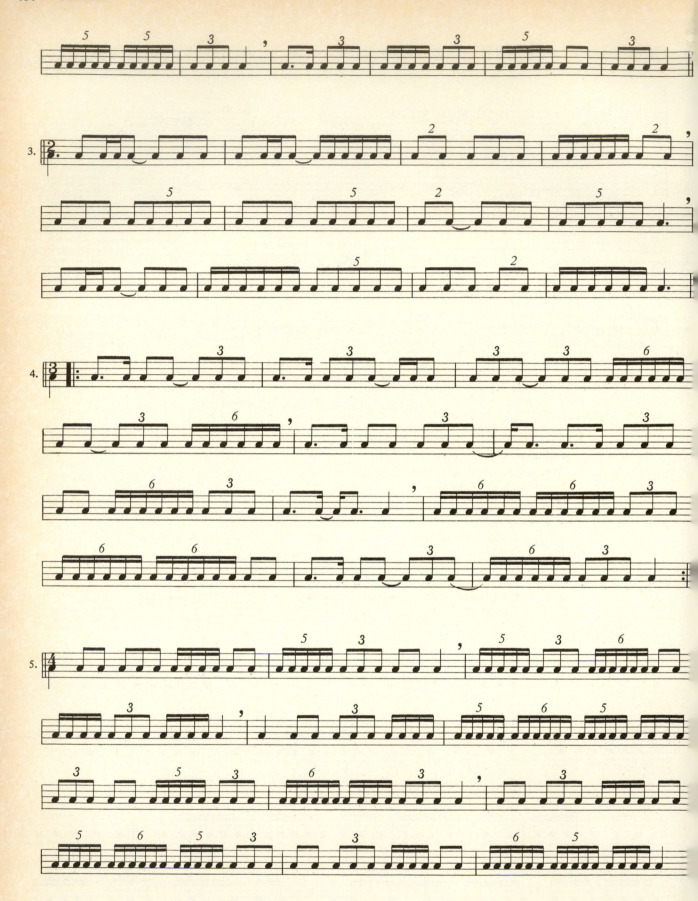

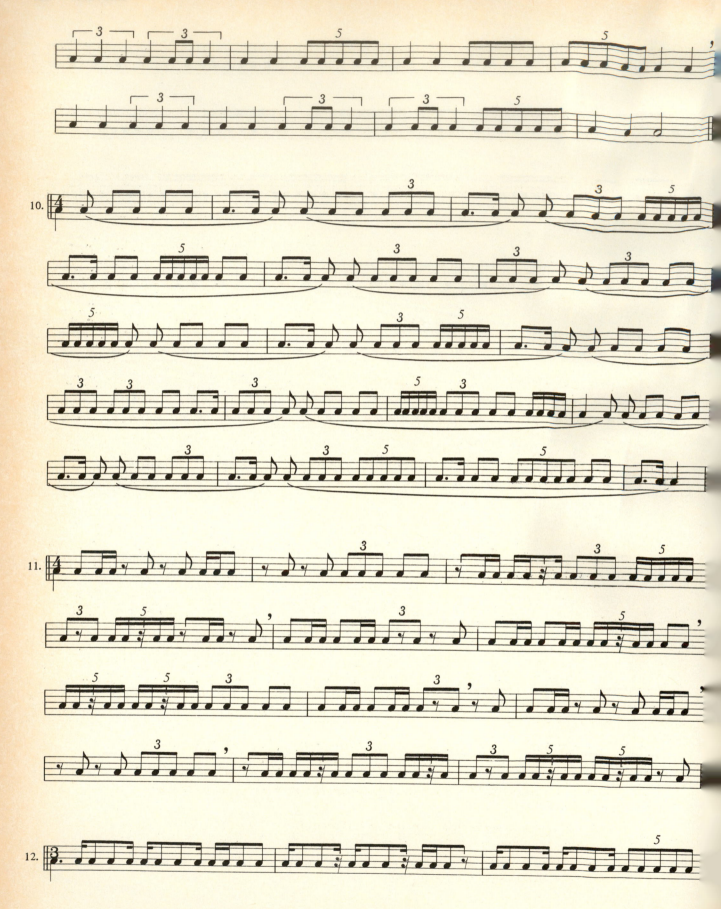

RHYTHM READING II

On each exercise perform the following tasks in the order given. Use a variety of tempi and dynamics.

1. Articulate the rhythm of each voice on neutral syllables while
    clapping the beat.
    clapping the divisions.
    employing the proper arm-beat patterns.

2. While employing the arm-beat patterns, improvise by

arbitrarily replacing the note values for rests.

singing a major and then a minor melody on each voice, using a variety of intervals and ending on tonic.

3. Sing a minor melody on the soprano voice using a variety of intervals and ending on tonic while clapping the rhythm of the bass voice.

4. Sing a minor melody on the soprano voice using a variety of intervals and ending on tonic while clapping the rhythm of the bass voice.

CLEF READING

On each exercise perform the tasks in the order given. Use a metronome, beginning at a slow tempo and increasing the rate of speed daily. Invent your own articulation for those exercises which are unedited.

1. Speak the rhythm on syllables that best produce the desired articulation while

   clapping the divisions.

   clapping the beat.

   employing the arm-beat pattern.

2. Speak (not sing) the letter name of each note out loud in the designated clefs while observing the correct articulation and using the proper arm-beat pattern.

MELODIES

Study each melody as to initial, middle (if applicable), and final tonalities. Find the best pivot tone(s) and mark on the music. Then sing the melody, using a neutral syllable, scale degree numbers, pitch names, or solfeggio syllables. If using scale degree numbers, change to the number for the new tonality on the pivot tone.

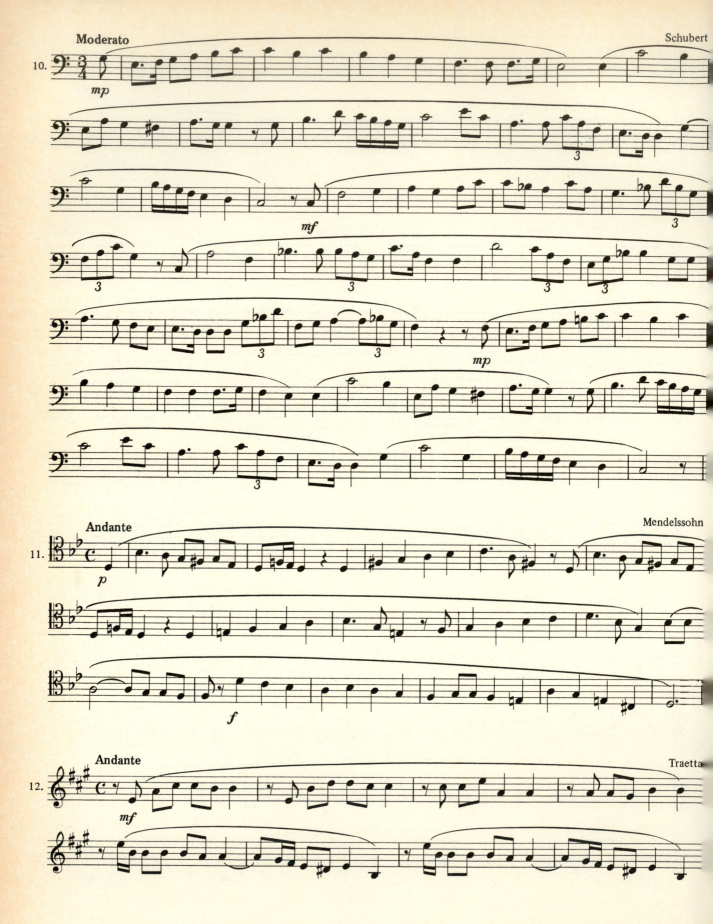

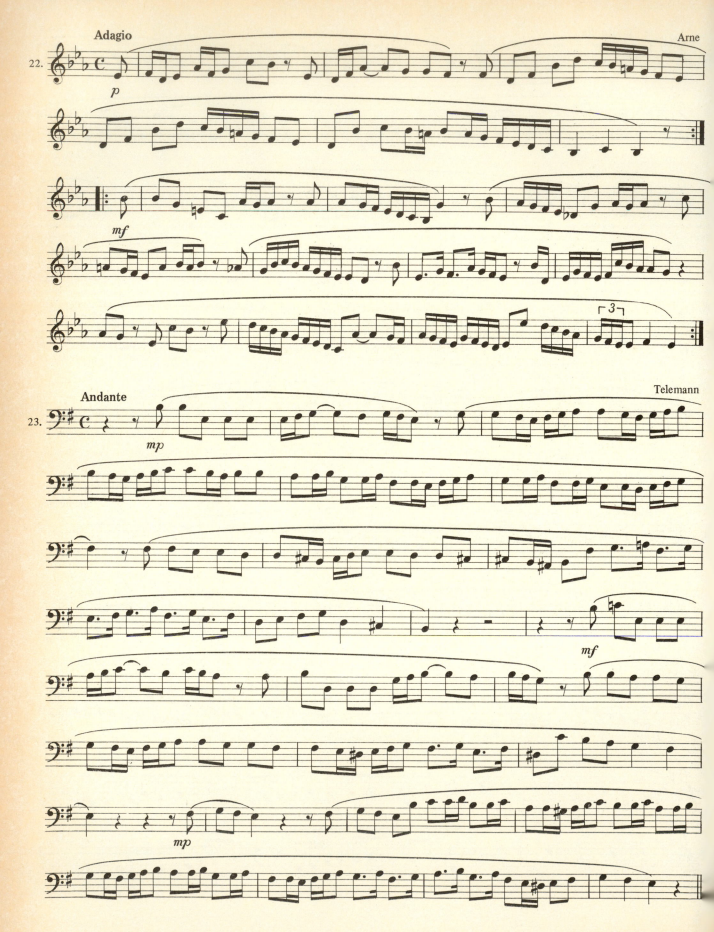

DUETS

1. Divide the class in half to perform duets.
2. Have two students perform the duets.
3. Sing one line and clap the rhythm of the other.
4. Sing one line and perform the other on the piano (play and sing).

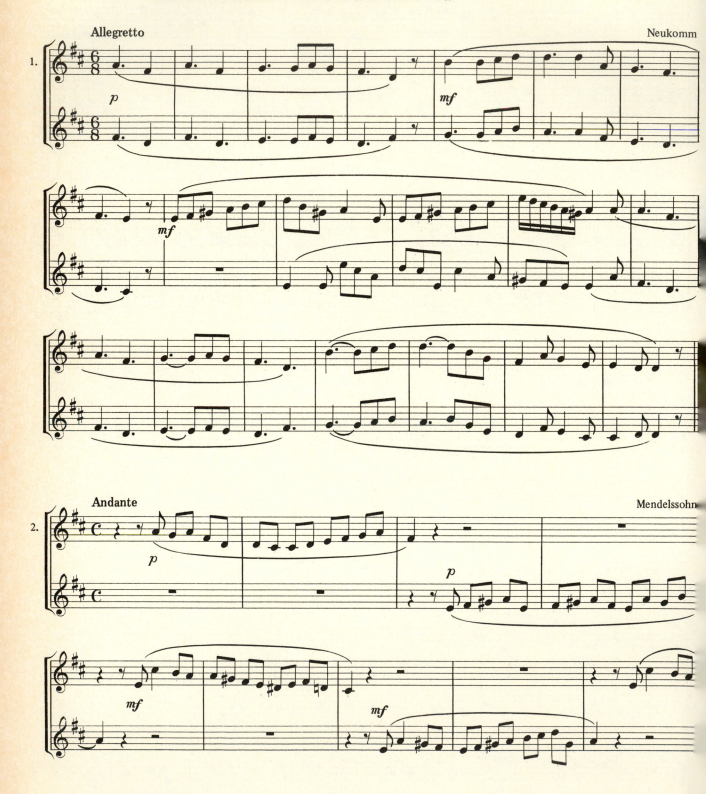

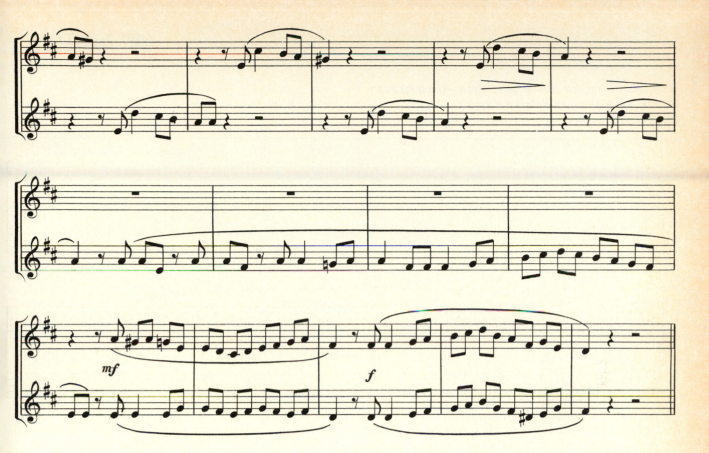

RHYTHM: *Complex (Composite) Meter—Unequal Beats*
PITCH: *Modualtion to Relative Keys*
CLEFS: *Treble, Bass, Tenor, Alto, and Two-Part Reading*

RHYTHM: *Complex (Composite) Meter—Unequal Beats*

Thus far in this text, the reader has experienced an in-depth study into simple and compound meter. These meters are considered to be *classic* metric structures, since each beat within the same measure is equidistant from the others. See examples 1a, b, and c.

This unit introduces an exploration into *Greek* metric structure, whereby beats within the measure are *not* always equidistant from the others. In Greek structure, beats may expand or contract, causing a physical sensation known as unequal beats. Meters that signify unequal beats are normally referred to as *complex* or *composite* meters. See examples 2a, b, and c, which illustrate three possible complex meters.

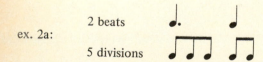

ex. 2b:

4 beats

12 divisions

ex. 2c:

3 beats

7 divisions

Since the beat-note value is not a constant within the measure, the meter signature cannot signify the number of beats per measure or the value of those beats. Traditionally, therefore, complex meter signatures (like compound meter signatures) are written to signify the number and quality of *divisions* per measure. Therefore, [♩. ♪ ♩] would be indicated as $\frac{5}{4}$ or $\frac{5}{♪}$.

With this method of metric notation, the reader is left to group the divisions into beats according to his or her own interpretation, based upon the composition's harmonic rhythm, melodic design, and rhythm pattern. Often, the eighth note or sixteenth note is used as the division note value, permitting the composer (or editor) to beam the note values together into beats such as [♪ ♪ ♪. ♪ ♪] or [♫ ♫ ♪] to visually aid the interpreter.

Once the beat structure is decided, the question remains: Does one use an arm-beat pattern depicting divisions or depicting beats? Throughout this text, the question has always been answered based upon the idea that one's arm-beat pattern depicts beats while demonstrating (through the style of gesture) the number of divisions per beat. Therefore, in the following examples, the arm-beat gestures used would be determined by the grouping of divisions. In examples 3a and 3b, a two-beat gesture would be used. In 3a, the first beat would be equal to a dotted quarter and the second, a quarter. This pattern is reversed in example 3b.

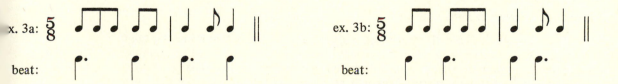

ex. 3a: $\frac{5}{8}$

beat:

ex. 3b: $\frac{5}{8}$

beat:

Examples 4a and 4b illustrate two possible groupings which can be found in $\frac{7}{8}$ meter. In each, a three-beat gesture is to be used. Example 4a is based on the beat pattern [♩ + ♩ + ♩.], while 4b is based on the pattern [♩. + ♩ + ♩].

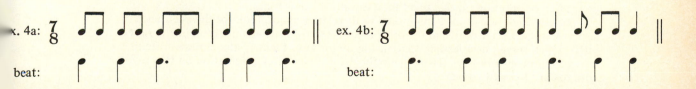

ex. 4a: $\frac{7}{8}$

beat:

ex. 4b: $\frac{7}{8}$

beat:

However, if the tempo is slow and the beat is divided and subdivided into complicated rhythm patterns, some musicians may feel a need to create gestures that show the divisions rather than the beats. Often the meters of $\frac{5}{4}$ and $\frac{7}{4}$ are those in question. In a meter of $\frac{5}{4}$ the divisions may be conducted in two different ways. See examples 5a and 5b.

ex. 5a: $\frac{5}{4}$

ex. 5b: $\frac{5}{4}$

A meter of $\frac{7}{4}$ would have these possibilities:

ex. 6a: $\frac{7}{4}$

ex. 6b: $\frac{7}{4}$

ex. 6c: $\frac{7}{4}$

PITCH: *Modulation to Relative Keys*

Relative keys can be defined as those major and minor keys that share the same key signature (the concept of related keys will be expanded in unit 16). For example, B♭ major and g minor are related since both have key signatures of two flats.

Modulations between relative keys will be comparatively simple since their key signatures are the same. Generally, modulations to relative keys will involve

1. a focus on a new pitch as tonic and
2. the addition or deletion of those chromatic pitches which, in minor, serve as the raised sixth and seventh scale degrees.

When modulating to relative keys, a pivot tone modulation will still be the most effective method to use. In a modulation from a major key to its relative minor, find the first chromatic alteration. This chromatic pitch will generally be the new leading tone. Identify the closest preceding note common to both keys. Then, mentally change your pitch orientation on that pivot tone toward the new tonic.

In a modulation from a minor key to its relative major, look for the occurence of a natural seventh scale degree in the original key. This will signal a negation of the raised pitch which served as a leading tone in the minor key. Identify the closest preceding note common to both keys. Then, mentally change your pitch orientation on that pivot note toward the new tonic.

PITCH EXERCISES

1. Establish the initial key by singing 1 3 5 3 1. Then perform the following modulating exercises on scale degree numbers. When reaching the pivot tone, repeat that pitch using both scale degree numbers.

   a. b minor: 1 2 3 4 5 6 5 8 7 6 5 3 4 2 | 1
                 D major: | 6 5 1 2 3 4 5 6 5 8 7 6 5 3 4 2 1

   b. A major: 8 7 8 5 3 ♯4 5 3 ♮4 2 3 4 5 ↓7 | 1
                 f♯ minor: | 3 5 8 ♯7 8 5 ↑1 3 5 4 3 1 2 ♯7 1

   c. g minor: 1 2 3 1 ♯7 1 ↓5 ↑3 2 1 ↑5 4 3 | 2
                 B♭ major: | 7 8 ↓5 ↓1 2 3 2 1 ↑5 6 4 5 7 8

   d. E♭ major: 1 ↑5 3 2 1 7 1 ↑5 6 5 8 7 6 4 5 | 3
              c minor: | 5 3 2 1 2 1 ♮7 1 ↑5 6 5 8 5 ↓♮7 1

2. Before beginning, study each melody as to initial, middle (if applicable), and final tonalities and determine which chromatic pitch(es) will imply a key change. Then, establish the initial key and perform each melody, filling in the blank measures with modulating material. Keep the new material rhythmically consistent with the rest of the melody.

3. Continue each of the following melodies in the established style, modulating to the specified key.

Improvise two more phrases modulating to b minor.

Improvise two more phrases modulating to F major.

Improvise two more phrases modulating to e minor.

PITCH PATTERNS

Study each pitch pattern to determine beginning and final tonalities. Choose a possible pivot tone and determine its scale degree function in each key. Then perform the pattern on a neutral syllable, scale degree numbers, pitch names, or solfeggio syllables. If using scale degree numbers, repeat the pivot note using scale degree numbers in both keys.

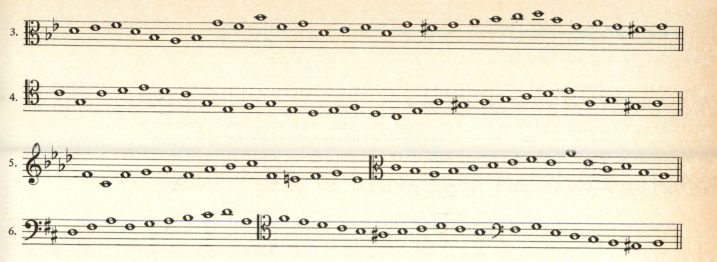

RHYTHM READING I

On each exercise perform the tasks in the order given. Use a variety of tempi and dynamics.

1. Articulate the rhythm on neutral syllables while

clapping the beat.

clapping the divisions.

employing the arm-beat pattern.

2. While employing the arm-beat pattern,

improvise on each exercise by arbitrarily replacing the note values with rests.

improvise a major melody and then a minor melody using a variety of intervals and ending on tonic. Use a variety of tonalities.

RHYTHM READING II

On each exercise perform the tasks in the order given. Use a variety of tempi and dynamics.

1. Articulate the rhythm of each voice on neutral syllables while

   clapping the beat.

   clapping the divisions.

   employing the proper arm-beat patterns

2. While employing the arm-beat patterns, improvise by

   arbitrarily replacing the note values for rests.

   singing a major and then a minor melody on each voice using a variety of intervals and ending on tonic.

3. Sing a minor melody on the soprano voice using a variety of intervals and ending on tonic. Clap the rhythm of the bass voice.

TWO-PART CLEF READING

On each exercise perform the tasks in the order given. Use a metronome, beginning at a slow tempo and increasing the rate of speed daily. Invent your own articulation for the bottom voice of each exercise.

1. Speak the rhythm of each voice on syllables that best produce the desired articulation while
   clapping the beat.
   clapping the divisions.
   employing the arm-beat pattern.

2. Speak (not sing) the letter name of each note out loud in the designated clefs while observing the correct articulation. Clap the rhythm of the bottom voice.

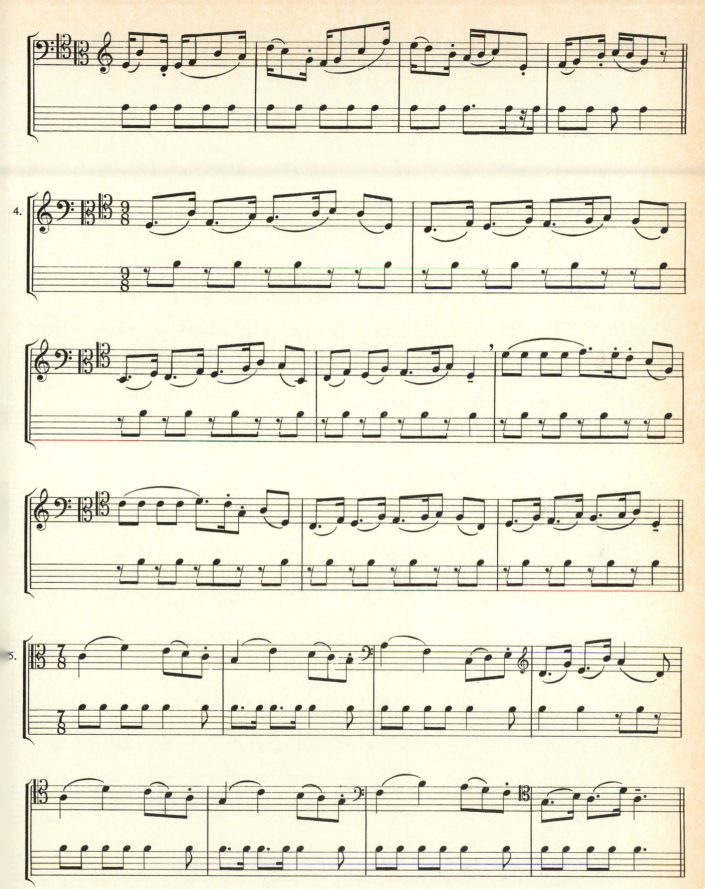

MELODIES

Study each melody as to initial, middle (if applicable), and final tonalities. Find the best pivot tone(s) and mark on the music. Then sing the melody, using a neutral syllable, scale degree numbers, pitch names, or solfeggio syllables. If using scale degree numbers, change to the number for the new tonality on the pivot tone.

Con brio

8.

Allegro

Couperin

9.

Allegretto mosso

Rimsky-Korsakov

10.

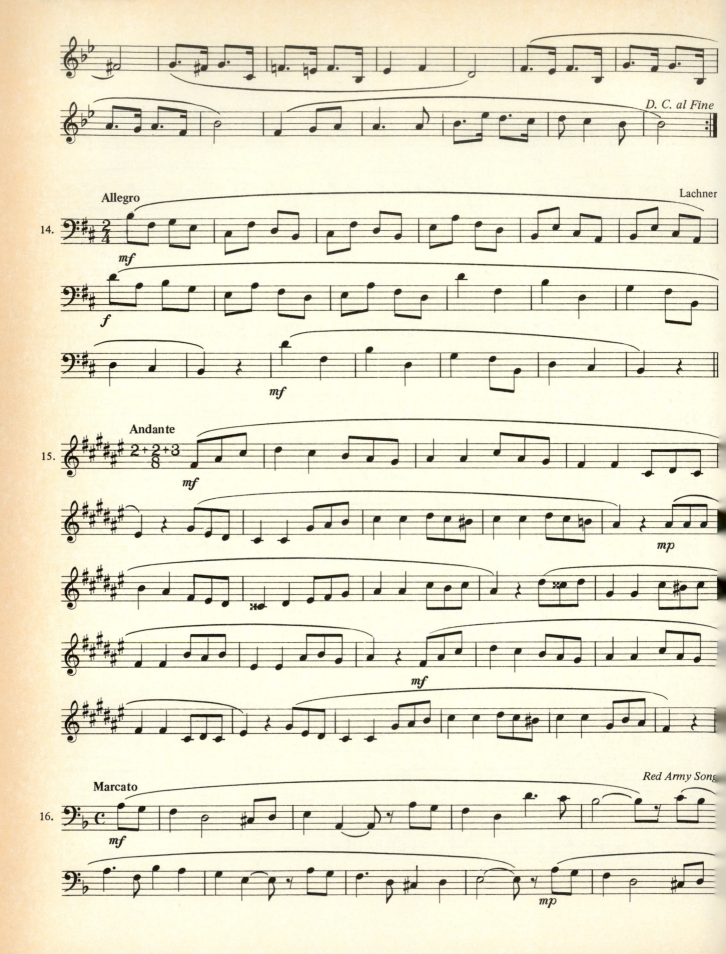

Andante — Haydn

17.

Andante — Schumann

18.

25. Grave   Telemann

26. Presto   Matteis

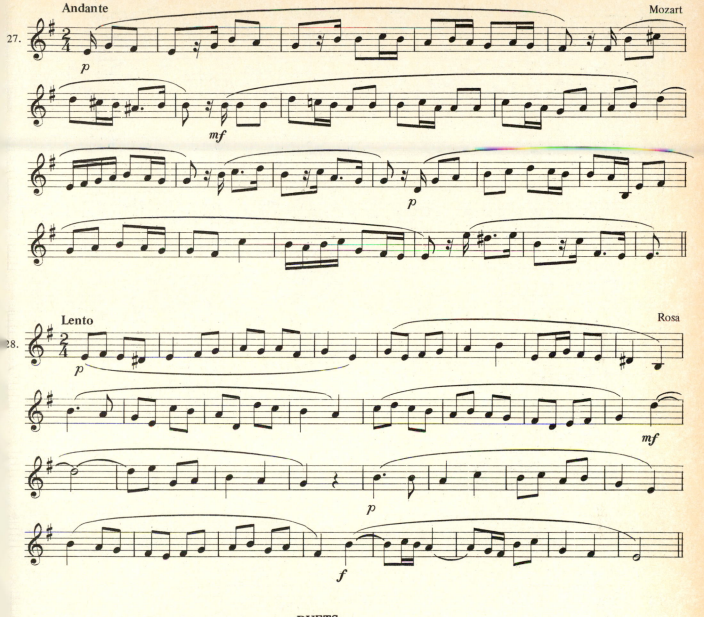

DUETS

1. Divide the class in half to perform duets.
2. Have two students perform duets.
3. Sing one line and clap the rhythm of the other.
4. Sing one line and perform the other on the piano.

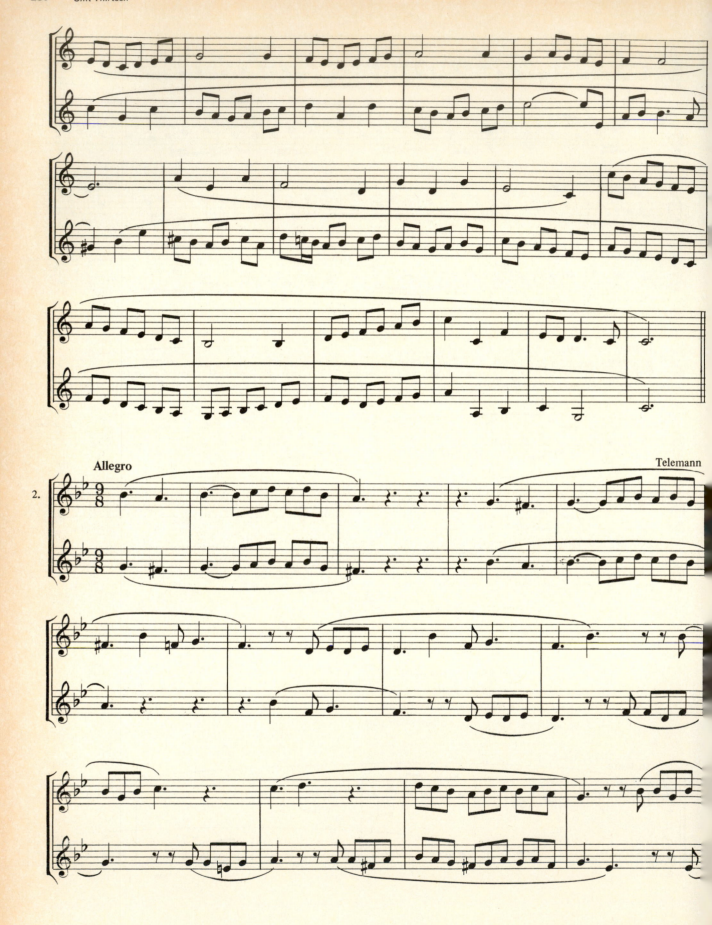

Allegro

Telemann

2.

RHYTHM: *Changing Meter (Simple/Compound/Complex)*
PITCH: *Modulation to Other Near-Related Keys*
CLEFS: *Treble, Bass, Alto, Tenor, and Two-Part Reading*

RHYTHM: *Changing Meter (Simple/Compound/Complex)*

Changing meter, as discussed in all previous units on the subject, implies that the crusic stresses within a given composition are not consistantly equidistant. In this unit, the reader will explore the change of meters in music that contains both Greek and Classic metric structure. This parenthetically implies the necessity for the use of metric indicators like those discussed in unit 9 (beat-to-beat and division-to-division) as well as metric indicators that show a beat-to-division and/or a division-to-beat relationship. Study the following examples.

$(♪=♪)$ indicates a beat (♩)-to-division (♪) relationship

$(♪=♩)$ indicates a division (♪)-to-beat (♩) relationship

PITCH: *Modulation to Other Near-Related Keys*

Near-related keys can be defined as those whose key signatures differ by no more than one sharp or flat. For example, the key of A major, with three sharps in its key signature, is related to all those major and minor keys which have two, three, or four sharps in their key signatures. The chart below illustrates this.

NEAR-RELATED KEYS TO A MAJOR

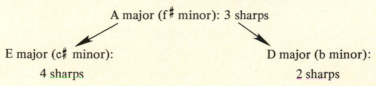

A major (f# minor): 3 sharps

E major (c# minor):   D major (b minor):

4 sharps   2 sharps

If the A major scale is written out and a diatonic triad is built on each scale degree from one to six, one can see that all of the preceding keys correspond to the major and minor chords found in this key.

I	ii	iii	IV	V	vi
A	b	c♯	D	E	f♯

Two near-related keys which are often involved in modulations in tonal music are the subdominant (IV, iv) and the dominant (V, v), both of which were covered in unit 12. In addition, unit 13 dealt with modulations to relative keys, that is, from tonic to its submediant in major (I–vi) and from tonic to its mediant in minor (i–III). This unit will focus on modulations to the remaining near-related keys: from a major key to its supertonic or mediant (I–ii; I–iii) and from a minor key to its submediant or subtonic (i–VI; i–VII).

PITCH EXERCISES

1. Establish the initial key by singing 1 3 5 3 1. Then perform the following modulating exercises on scale degree numbers. When reaching the pivot tone, repeat that pitch using both scale degree numbers. Before beginning, determine which scale degree in the second key will be altered.

   a. D major: 1 2 3 4 5 3 4 5 6 5 8 6 5 4 | 5
       e minor: | 4 3 2 3 1 5 6 5 8 6 5 3 2♯7 1

   b. F major: 3 4 5 1 7 2 1 5 6 4 5 3 2 3 4 | 5
       a minor: | 3 2 1♭5 6 5 1♯7 1 3 5 4 2♯7 1

   c. c minor: 1 ♮7 1 3 5 6 5 8 ♮7 8 5 3 4 5 3 | 2
       B♭ major: | 3 5 4 3 1 8 7 8 5 4 2 3 4 5♭7 1

   d. a minor: 1 ♯7 1♭5♮2 1 2♭5♮3 2 1 3 5 4 5 | 1
       F major: | 3 2♭7 1♮5 6 3 4 2 3 1 2 7 1

2. Before beginning, study each melody as to initial and final tonalities and determine which chromatic pitch(es) will imply a key change. Then, establish the initial key and perform each melody, filling in the blank measures with modulating material. Keep the new material rhythmically consistent with the rest of the melody.

3. Continue each of the following melodies in the established style, modulating to the specified key. Before beginning, determine the necessary chromatic change(s) and their relationship to both the initial and final key centers. Be sure to establish the second key.

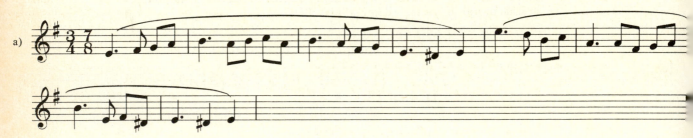

Improvise two more phrases modulating to C major.

Improvise two more phrases modulating to A major.

Improvise two more phrases modulating to d minor. Keep the pattern of meter changes consistent.

PITCH PATTERNS

Study each pitch pattern to determine beginning and final tonalities. Choose a possible pivot tone and determine its scale degree function in each key. Then perform the pattern on a neutral syllable, scale degree numbers, pitch names, or solfeggio syllables. If using scale degree numbers, repeat the pivot note using the number in both keys.

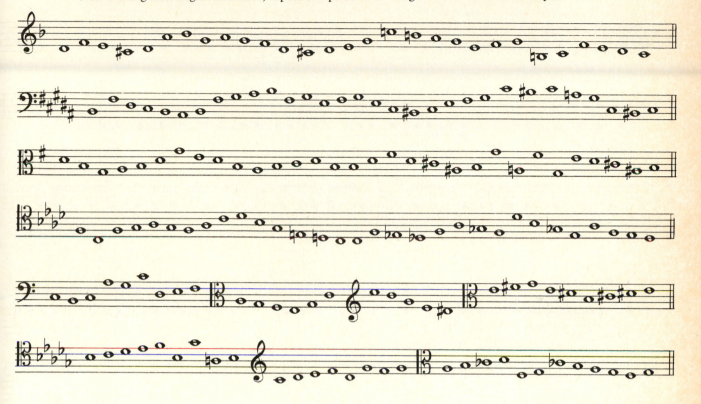

RHYTHM READING I

On each exercise perform the tasks in the order given. Use a variety of tempi and dynamics.

1. Articulate the rhythm on neutral syllables while
   clapping the beat.
   clapping the divisions.
   employing the arm-beat pattern.

2. While employing the arm-beat pattern,
   improvise on each exercise by arbitrarily replacing the note values for rests.
   improvise a major and then a minor melody using a variety of intervals and ending on tonic.
   Replace beats with rests and use a variety of tonalities.

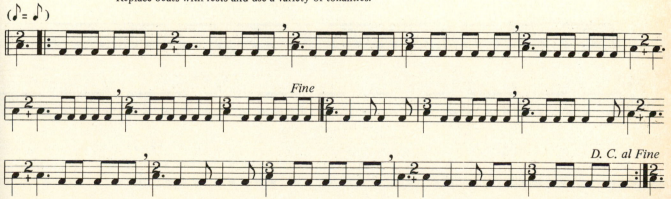

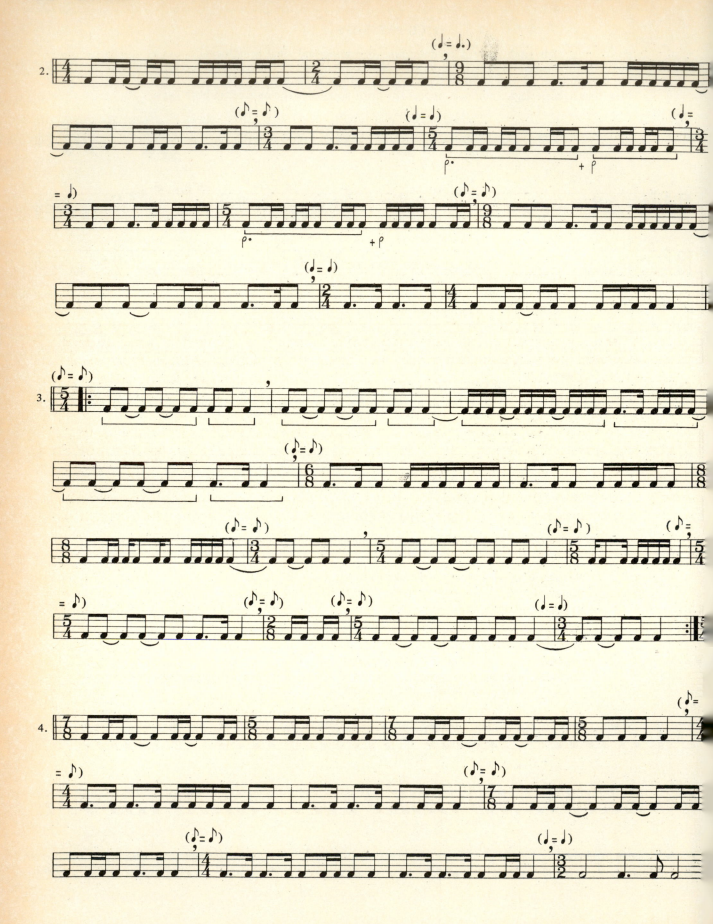

RHYTHM READING II

On each exercise perform the tasks in the order given. Use a variety of tempi and dynamics.

1. Articulate the rhythm of each voice on neutral syllables while
    clapping the beat.
    clapping the divisions.
    employing the proper arm-beat patterns.
2. While employing arm-beat patterns, improvise by
    arbitrarily replacing the note values for rests.
    singing a major and then a minor melody on each voice using a variety of intervals and ending on tonic.
3. Sing a minor melody on the soprano voice using a variety of intervals and ending on tonic.
    Clap the rhythm of the bass voice.

TWO-PART CLEF READING

On each exercise perform the tasks in the order given. Use a metronome, beginning at a slow tempo and increasing the rate of speed daily. Invent your own articulation for the bottom voice of each exercise.

1. Speak the rhythm of each voice on syllables that best produce the desired articulation while
   clapping the beat.
   clapping the divisions.
   employing the arm-beat patterns.

2. Speak (not sing) the letter name of each note out loud in the designated clefs of the upper voice while observing the correct articulation. Clap the rhythm of the bottom voice.

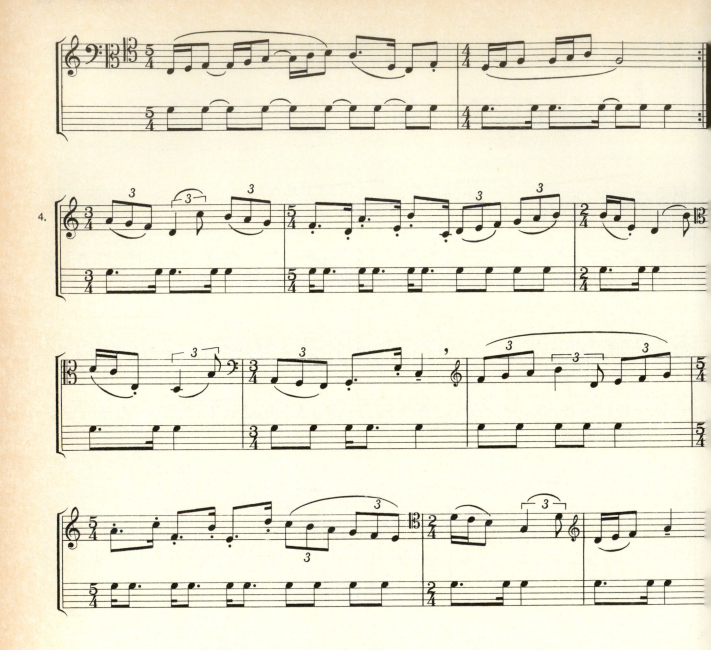

MELODIES

1. Study each melody to determine tonalities. Find the best pivot tone(s) and mark on the music. Then sing the melody, using a neutral syllable, scale degree numbers, pitch names, or solfeggio syllables. If using scale degree numbers, change to the number for the new tonality on the pivot tone.

2. In the melodies that contain changing meters (simple/compound/complex), decide your method of conducting (beat or division or combination) before beginning.

Allegro agitato   Tchaikovsky

N6 chord ——————— V

Allegro assai vivace   Mendelssohn

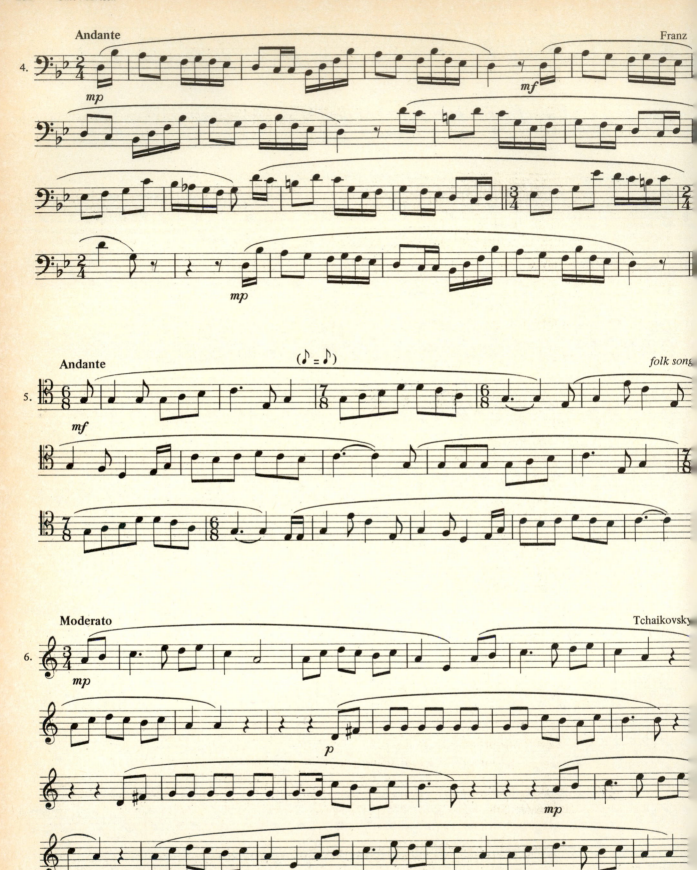

Andante cantabile

Leuto

11.

p

Allegro

English folk song

12.

mf

Allegro

Brahms

13.

mf

DUETS

1. Divide the class in half to perform the duet.
2. Have two students perform the duet.
3. Sing one line and clap the rhythm of the other.
4. Sing one line and perform the other at the piano.

Tchaikovsky

RHYTHM: *Poly-Metrics*
PITCH: *Distant and Transient Modulations*
CLEFS: *Treble, Bass, Tenor, Alto, and Two-Part Reading*

RHYTHM: *Poly-Metrics*

Poly-metrics is a term implying the use of two or more *superimposed meters* within one composition. Only meters that have the same number of divisions but whose divisions are grouped differently into beats are able to be superimposed upon each other. The following examples are offered as possible combinations, even though examples 1 and 2 are the only types of poly-metrics dealt with in this unit.

ex. 1:
| 2 beats (compound)
| 6 divisions
| 3 beats (simple)

ex. 2:
| 3 beats (simple)
| 12 divisions
| 4 beats (compound)

ex. 3:
| 3 beats (complex)
| 7 divisions
| 3 beats (complex)

ex. 4:
| 3 beats (compound)
| 8 divisions
| 4 beats (simple)

While performing poly-metric compositions it is vital to maintain the individual personality or integrity of each metric structure. When confronted with poly-metrics, one is often tempted to solve the metric conflict through the reduction of the beats to a *composite rhythm*. Examples 5a and 5b show how one arrives at the composite rhythm.

ex. 5a: = compound composite rhythm

= simple composite rhythm

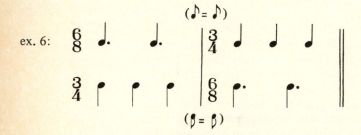

ex. 5b:

While serving as a good check for accuracy, the use of these composite rhythms for the *execution* of the composition will cause the two opposing metric personalities to merge into one, and this merger always destroys the polyphonic effect.

All of the rhythm exercises contained in this unit are in two parts. In addition, many exercises also contain changing meter. As usual, these metric changes are effected through a relationship of division equals division and/or beat equals beat (see unit 9). When changing meter is employed in this unit, the voices will always exchange their roles. Therefore, when a division-to-division relationship is maintained, the effect is that one hears the bass voice move to the soprano and the soprano voice move to the bass (see example 6).

ex. 6:

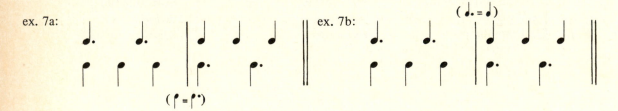

However, when a beat-to-beat relationship is employed, the effect is very different. One perceives a definite exchange of roles but, in addition, the tempo of each of the voices is changed. Study examples 7a and 7b, where two possibilities of this change in tempo are illustrated.

ex. 7a: ex. 7b:

In example 7a, the indicator states that the tempo of the quarter note in measure one (bass voice) is to be maintained for the dotted quarter note in measure two. Therefore, the tempo of the quarter note in measure two (soprano voice) will be faster than the tempo of the quarter note in measure one (bass voice). This creates an overall increase in tempo. Example 7b illustrates how the indicator affects the soprano voice and thereby creates an overall decrease in tempo.

PITCH: *Distant and Transient Modulations*

Distant keys can be defined as those which are not near-related. That is, they are all those keys having key signatures containing more or less than one sharp or flat than the original key.

When studying modulations to distant keys, generally a pivot tone can be found. However, a careful study of those key changes can uncover many other factors, an understanding of which can make the melodies easier to perform. Melody 2 on page 267 involves a change from A major to G major. In measure four, there is a simple pivot tone modulation where *b* is the pivot tone and the C♮ in the following measure is the chromatic inflection which acts as the dominant in the new key.

Another example that illustrates different types of modulations is melody 5 on page 268. In measure twenty-four there is a cadence on the dominant in the key of E♭ major followed by a direct *shift* to a new tonic note, F♯. The return to the key of E♭ begins nine measures later with an enharmonic respelling of the notes F♯ → G♯ → A♯ as B♭ → A♭ → G♭. These pitches then assume the role of 5–4–3 in the key of e♭ minor, and later there is a mutation to the original major mode.

Other modulations to distant keys found in this unit involve such techniques as modulating sequence, chromatic inflection, and common tone. Each melody should be carefully studied to determine location and method of each key change before singing.

Music that involves *transient modulations* will generally contain changes to several temporary keys, each of which is well established before moving on to the next tonal center. This music will be easier to sing in the sense that the keys usually will be closely related to the adjacent keys. However, the fact that the tonal centers are constantly changing will create the need for additional analysis and reading ahead. Each melody in the transient modulations section should be carefully studied to determine the various key centers before singing.

PITCH EXERCISES

1. The following patterns all contain modulations to distant keys using pivot notes as the method of modulation. Before singing each, determine the initial chromatic changes which will have to be made in the second key. Then perform, repeating the pivot note on both scale degree numbers.

    a. A major: 3 4 5 6 5 3 1 2 3 5 8 7 6 5 4 |3
        D♭ major: |1 2 3 1 3 4 5 6 5 8 7 6 5↓7 1

    b. e♭ minor: 3 2 3 4 5 1 6 4 5 8 7 6 5 3 1 2| 1
        B major: |3 2 1 5 8 5 3 4 2 1

    c. E major: 5 6 5 3 4 2 1 3 5 6 5 8 7 6 5 3 |1
        F major: |7 2 1 3 5 8 7 8 6 5 6 4 5↓7 1

    d. B♭ major: 1 2 3 1 3 4 5 3 4 2 1 7 1 3 2 |3
        D major: |1 2 3 5 8 7 8 5 4 3 2 1 2 7 1

2. The following is a list of pairs of distantly related keys. In each pair of keys, identify a possible pivot note which is common to both keys. Then, improvise a pitch pattern that illustrates a modulation using that pivot note.

    a. A♭ major - b minor   **c.** E major - B♭ major

    b. a minor - f♯ minor   **d.** g minor - A major

3. Using the following as the first phrase of a three-phrase melody, continue the melody by improvising four different second phrases that illustrate the types of modulations described below. Continue the melody by establishing the new key in the third phrase.

    a. a modulation to b minor using a common tone d

    b. a modulation by direct shift to the key of A♭ major

    c. a modulation to the key of E major achieved by introducing a chromatic inflection of the note d to d♯

    d. a modulation to g minor via the mutation of the dominant chord in C major

4. The following melody involves several modulations to transient key centers. Use the blank measures to improvise modulatory material leading to the subsequent keys.

PITCH PATTERNS

Before singing the following pitch patterns, determine the initial and final tonalities and the method of modulation. Then, perform the patterns, using scale degree numbers, neutral syllables, pitch names, or solfeggio syllables.

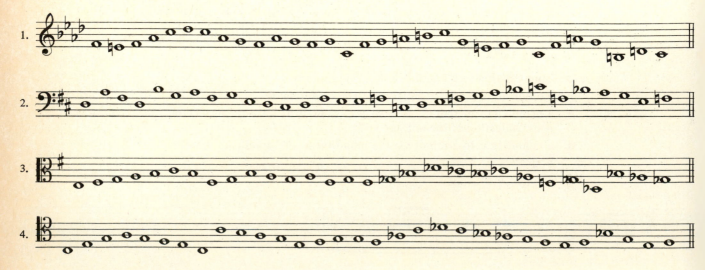

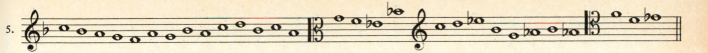

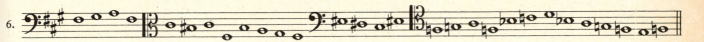

RHYTHM READING I

The following exercises contain only beat patterns of one meter against another. This is done so that the student gains practice in maintaining the character of meters while against one another before adding rhythm. In the order given and using neutral syllables the student should

  1. articulate each voice while using the arm-beat patterns.
  2. articulate each voice while clapping the other.
  3. articulate each voice while employing the arm-beat pattern for the other.

If the student wishes she/he may continue by

  4. performing the arm-beat pattern for the top voice with the right arm and performing the the arm-beat pattern for the bottom voice with the left arm.
  5. repeating step 4 while improvising rhythm in either meter through vocal articulation on neutral syllables.

RHYTHM READING II

In this section, rhythm has been added to the top voice while the beat pattern of the opposite meter is held in the bass voice. In the order given and on neutral syllables, the student should

1. articulate the rhythm of the upper voice while using arm beats.
2. articulate the rhythm of the upper voice while clapping the bottom voice.
3. improvise a major and/or a minor melody on the top voice while using arm beats for the meter of the bottom voice.

If the student wishes she/he may continue by

4. employing the arm-beat pattern of the top voice with the right arm and, with the left arm, employing the arm-beat pattern of the bottom voice.
5. repeating step 4 above while improvising a major and/or a minor melody on the rhythm of the top voice. Use neutral syllables and end on tonic.

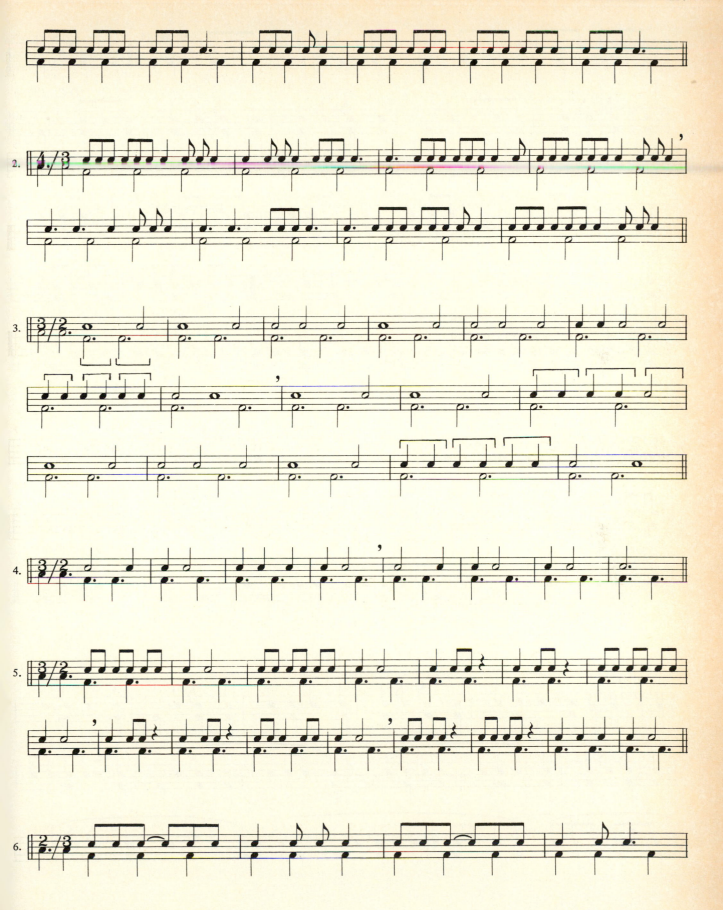

RHYTHM READING III

In this section, rhythm is used in both voices. In the order given and on neutral syllables, the student should

1. articulate the rhythm of each voice while using the arm-beat pattern.
2. articulate the rhythm of the top voice while clapping the rhythm of the bottom voice.
3. improvise a major and/or a minor melody on the top voice while clapping the rhythm of the bottom voice.

TWO-PART CLEF READING

On each exercise perform the tasks in the order given. Use a metronome, beginning at a slow tempo and increasing the rate of speed daily. Invent your own articulation for the bottom voice of each exercise.

1. Speak the rhythm of each voice on syllables that will best produce the desired articulation while

   clapping the beat.

   clapping the divisions.

   employing the arm-beat pattern.

2. Speak (not sing) the letter name of each note out loud in the designated clefs of the upper voice while observing the correct articulation. Clap the rhythm of the bottom voice.

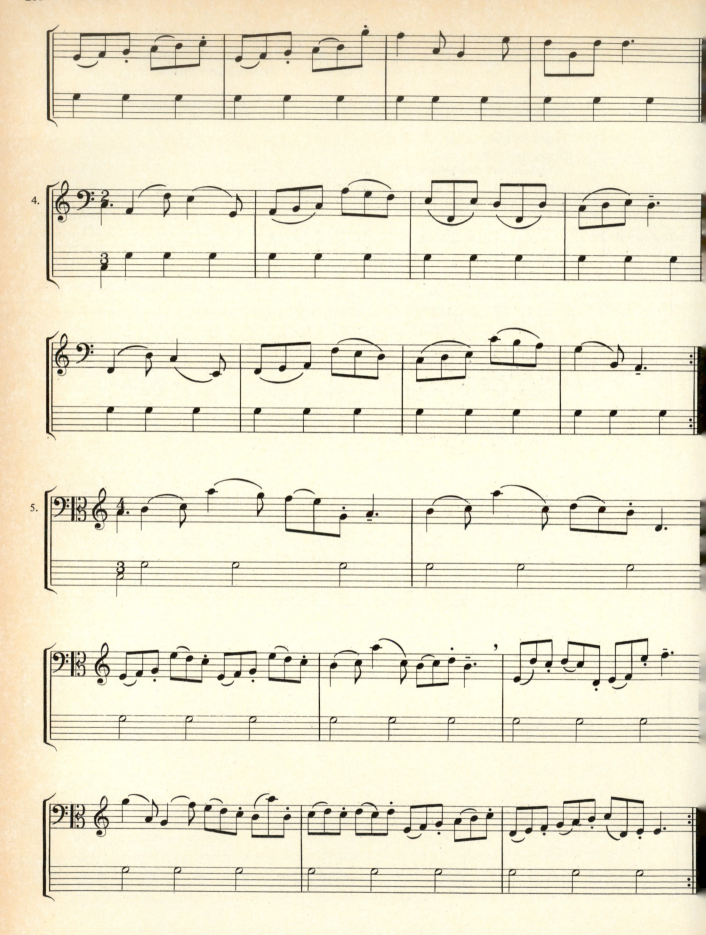

MELODIES

Study each melody to determine tonalities. Determine the location and the method of the modulation and mark it on the music. Then sing the melody, using neutral syllables, scale degree numbers, pitch names, or solfeggio syllables.

Modulations to Distant Keys

Transient Modulations

13. Larghetto   Bianchi

Allegretto   Caccini

17.

DUETS

1. Divide the class in half to perform duets.
2. Have two students perform duets.
3. Sing one line and clap the rhythm of the other.
4. Sing one line and perform the other on the piano.

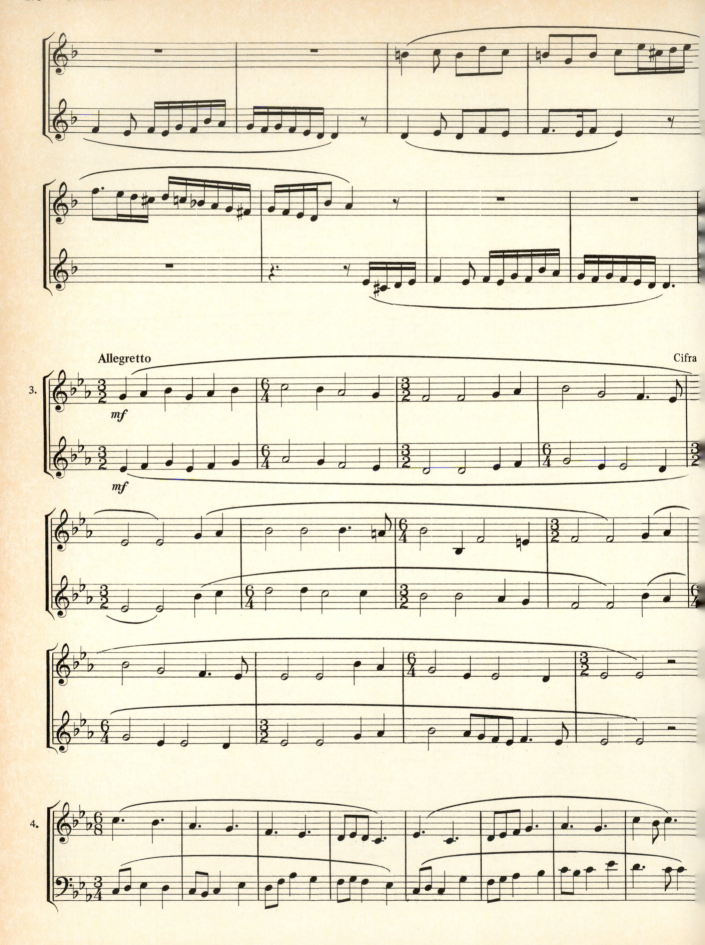

RHYTHM: *Metric and Rhythmic Transformation*
PITCH: *The Modes*
CLEFS: *A Review*

RHYTHM: *Metric and Rhythmic Transformation*

The term *transformation*, when referring to meter, implies that the composer or improvisator who is working with a given number of divisions per measure has decidedly regrouped that same number of divisions per measure into a different number of beats. For example, the meter of $\frac{3}{4}$ containing 6 divisions and 3 beats could be regrouped into a meter of $\frac{6}{8}$, which also contains 6 divisions but only 2 beats. See example 1.

ex. 1:

Likewise, when referring to rhythm, the term transformation implies that the composer or improvisator who is working with a given rhythmic pattern or phrase has decidedly reworked the same pattern or phrase into a transformable metric structure. See example 2.

ex. 2:

Example 2 shows a rhythmic transformation of the pattern "quarter 2 eighths quarter," which happens to be the composite rhythm of $\frac{3}{4}$ against $\frac{6}{8}$ (see unit 15). In fact, all rhythms that are composites of poly–metrics can be transformed into either metric structure. Study the following chart of composite rhythms.

2 Against 3 or 3 Against 2

3 beats with 2 divisions each

2 beats with 3 divisions each

3 Against 4 or 4 Against 3

4 beats with 3 divisions each

3 beats with 4 divisions each

5 Against 2, 3, and 4, or 2, 3, and 4 Against 5

5 beats with 2 divisions each

2 beats with 5 divisions each

5 beats with 3 divisions each

3 beats with 5 divisions each

5 beats with 4 divisions each

4 beats with 5 divisions each

note: observe that all composite rhythms are mirror images when viewed from the center (*).

Finally, it is not to be implied that only composite rhythms are transformable. Any rhythm in ¾ or ⁶⁄₈ is transformable to the other meter. Furthermore, any rhythm in ⁴⁄♩., ³⁄♩, ⁶⁄♪, or ²⁄♩. is transformable to any of the other meters. The authors have composed several exercises on this subject and trust that both the teacher and student will enjoy performing them and exploring the concept in preceding units or in their own composition and improvisation.

PITCH: *The Modes*

In addition to major and minor, there are many different arrangements of half and whole steps which create other scales or *modes*. Until the major and minor scales became popular in the seventeenth century, much music was written in these Medieval or Church modes. Since that time, many composers have returned to the use of these other scales as a basis for their music, and these other modes can be found particularly in folk music of all periods and countries, Eastern European music of composers such as Tchaikovsky, and impressionistic and contemporary composers such as Debussy, Ravel, Bartók, and Stravinsky.

If a major scale is constructed and then new scales written beginning on each scale degree of that major scale, the structure of the modes can be seen. Note the new position of the half steps in the following scales.

Ionian (major)   Dorian

In identifying and singing melodies in the various modes, it is beneficial to think of the unfamiliar modes in relation to major and minor (aeolian). The following examples illustrate these relationships.

1. The lydian scale is similar to the major scale but has a raised fourth scale degree.

F major   F lydian

2. The mixolydian scale is similar to the major scale but has a lowered seventh scale degree.

F major   F mixolydian

3. The dorian scale is similar to the aeolian scale but has a raised sixth scale degree.

f aeolian   f dorian

4. The phrygian scale is similar to the aeolian scale but has a lowered second scale degree.

f aeolian   f phrygian

5. The locrian scale is rarely used in tonal music because of its lack of a strong tonal framework. The interval of the perfect fifth which exists between the first and fifth scale degrees in all of the other scales is a diminished fifth in the locrian scale.

PITCH EXERCISES

1. Practice singing scales in the following ways:
   a. Using scale degree numbers, sing a major scale, then lydian and mixolydian, using the same note as tonic.
   b. Using scale degree numbers, sing an aeolian scale, then dorian and phrygian, using the same note as tonic.
   c. Using different notes as tonic, sing various modal scales. Use scale degree numbers, a neutral syllable and pitch names.
2. Sing the following patterns in each of the following modes: ionian, lydian, mixolydian, aeolian, dorian, and phrygian.

   a. tonic: a   1 3 5 6 8 7 6 5 3 4 5 1
   b. tonic: e   5 6 5 3 4 5 4 2 3 5 1 2 7 1
   c. tonic: f♯   3 2 1 5 6 4 5 7 1↓5↑3 2 7 1
   d. tonic: b   5 3 1 2 3 4 5 8 7 5 6 4 5 1

PITCH PATTERNS

Study each pattern to determine tonic and mode. Then establish tonic and perform the pattern using scale degree numbers, a neutral syllable, pitch names, or solfeggio syllables.

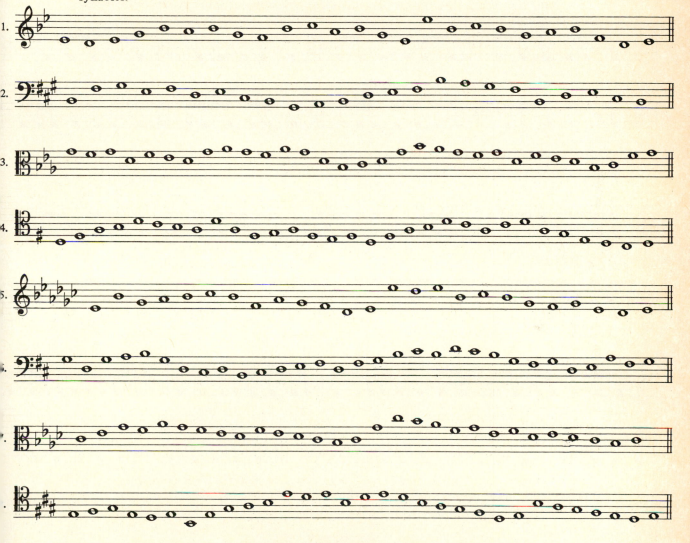

RHYTHM READING I
Rhythmic Transformation I

1. On each exercise and in the order given, articulate the rhythm on neutral syllables while performing the following tasks. In the blank measures, transform the rhythm of the previous measure.

   Clap the divisions.

   Clap the beats.

   Use arm–beat patterns.

2. While employing the arm-beat pattern, improvise a major and/or a minor melody on neutral syllables while using dynamics. End on tonic.

RHYTHM READING II
Rhythmic Transformation II

1. Transform each exercise into the other meter. If necessary, use paper and pencil.
2. Practice each exercise as written and then in the transformed meter by going through each step and procedure suggested in Rhythm Reading I.

TWO-PART CLEF READING
A Review

On each exercise, perform the tasks in the order given. Use a metronome, beginning at a slow tempo and increasing the rate of speed daily. Invent your own articulation for the bottom voice of each exercise.

1. Speak the rhythm of each voice on syllables that best produce the desired articulation while clapping the beat.

   clapping the divisions.

   employing the arm-beat pattern.

2. Speak (not sing) the letter name of each note out loud in the designated clefs of the upper voice while observing the correct articulation. Clap the rhythm of the bottom voice.

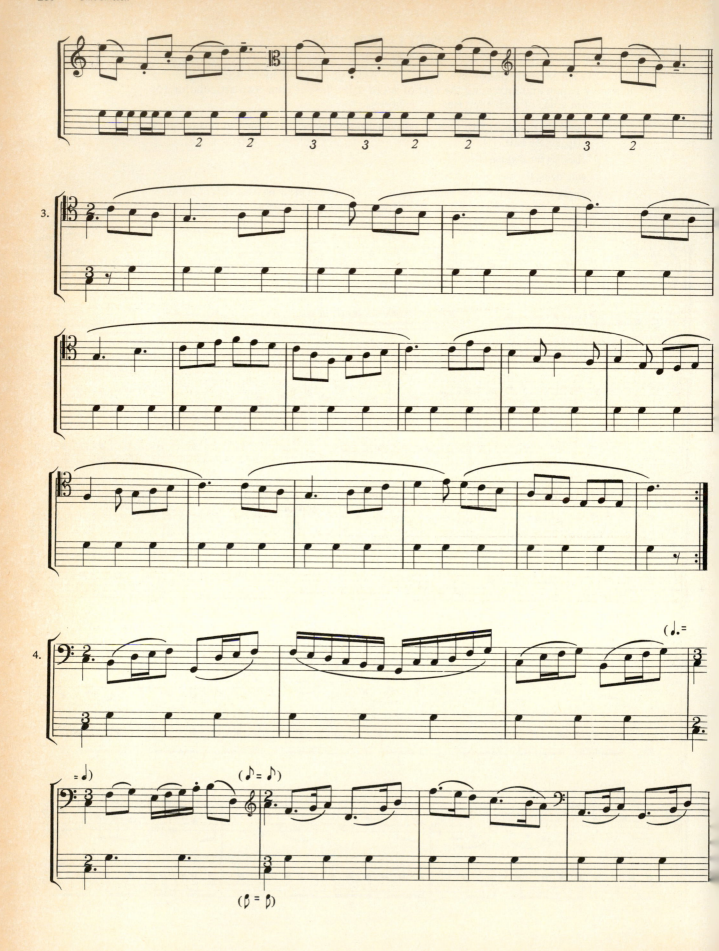

MELODIES

Study each melody to determine tonic and mode. Then establish tonic and perform each melody using neutral syllables, scale degree numbers, or pitch names.

Tchaikovsky

Poitou

23. Allegro — Tchaikovsky

24. Moderato — English folk song

25. Spirited — folk song

DUETS

1. Divide the class in half to perform duets.
2. Have two students perform the duets.
3. Sing one line and clap the rhythm of the other.
4. Sing one line and perform the other on the piano.

1. Andante — Ludford

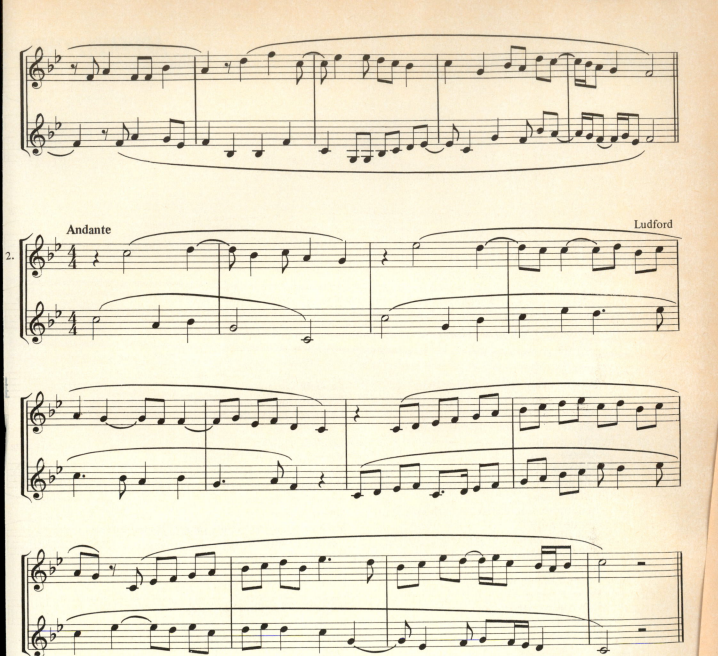

Andante

Ludford

2.

GLOSSARY OF FOREIGN TERMS

Adagio slow tempo, slower than Andante, faster than Largo
Agitato agitated, excited
Allegretto moderately fast, between Allegro and Andante
Allegro fast, quick
Amoroso lovingly
Andante moderate, between Allegretto and Adagio
Andantino somewhat faster than Andante
Anima spirit
Animato animated, spirited
Appassionata impassioned
Assai very
Ausdrucksvoll expressively
Bewegt agitated
Brio spirit, vigor
Cantabile in a singing style
Con with
Da capo (D.C.) from the beginning
Deciso bold
Dolce sweet and soft
Dolente sad, doleful
Espressivo expressive
Etwas somewhat
Fine end
Frisch brisk, lively
Fröhlich joyful, happy
Fuoco fire
Giocoso playful
Grave slow, solemn
Grazioso graceful
Innig heartfelt, ardent
Je port amiablement amiably
Langsam slow
Largo very slow and broad

Lebhaft animated
Legato smooth and connected
Leggiero light, graceful
Lento slow
Lieblich in a loving manner
Maestoso majestic, dignified
Ma non troppo but not too much
Marcato decisive, marked
Mässig moderate
Mesto sad, mournful
Moderato at a moderate tempo, between Andante and Allegro
Molto very much
Mosso motion
Moto motion
Nicht zu not too
Piacevole graceful, agreeable
Poco a little
Presto fast, quicker than Allegro
Primo first
Risoluto firm, resolute
Ruhig calm, tranquil
Schnell fast, quick
Sehr very
Sempre always
Sostenuto sustained
Spirito spirit
Tempo rate of speed
Tempo di Valse in the tempo of a Waltz (usually in one)
Teneramente tenderly
Tenerezza tenderness
Vif lively
Vivace quick, lively
Vivo quick, lively

AN INTEGRATED APPROACH TO SIGHTSINGING

RHYTHM

AND

PITCH

JOHN R. STEVENSON
MARJORIE S. PORTERFIELD

In this sightsinging book, the authors cover concepts in rhythm and pitch as well as skill development in music reading. Their integrated approach begins with simple melodic and rhythmic elements and progresses to complex rhythmic and tonal melodic material.

In each chapter there is an explanation of the theory of rhythm and pitch together with rhythm reading, clef reading, pitch exercises, and music for sightsinging.

Melodic and rhythmic exercises of improvisation, from a wide variety of styles, are introduced early in the book and developed throughout.

There are special chapters on complementary rhythm, hemiola, rhythmic transformation, poly-metrics, and changing meter. Other chapters cover chromatic non-chord tones, distant and transient modulations, and modes.

PRENTICE-HALL, INC., Englewood Cliffs, N.J. 07632

ISBN 0-13-780743-0